Conversations with Calvin

Conversations with Calvin

DAILY DEVOTIONS

Donald K. McKim

CASCADE *Books* • Eugene, Oregon

CONVERSATIONS WITH CALVIN
Daily Devotions

Copyright © 2019 Donald K. McKim. All rights reserved. Except for brief quotations in critical publications or reviews, no part of this book may be reproduced in any manner without prior written permission from the publisher. Write: Permissions, Wipf and Stock Publishers, 199 W. 8th Ave., Suite 3, Eugene, OR 97401.

Cascade Books
An Imprint of Wipf and Stock Publishers
199 W. 8th Ave., Suite 3
Eugene, OR 97401

www.wipfandstock.com

PAPERBACK ISBN: 978-1-5326-5097-0
HARDCOVER ISBN: 978-1-5326-5098-7
EBOOK ISBN: 978-1-5326-5099-4

Cataloguing-in-Publication data:

Names: McKim, Donald K., author.

Title: Conversations with Calvin : daily devotions / Donald K. McKim.

Description: Eugene, OR: Cascade Books, 2019 | Includes bibliographical references.

Identifiers: ISBN 978-1-5326-5097-0 (paperback) | ISBN 978-1-5326-5098-7 (hardcover) | ISBN 978-1-5326-5099-4 (ebook)

Subjects: LCSH: Calvin, Jean—1509–1564 | Spiritual life | Religious life | Theology, Doctrinal | Pastoral theology

Classification: BX9418 M35 2019 (print) | BX9418 (ebook)

Manufactured in the U.S.A.　　　　　　　　　　SEPTEMBER 4, 2019

For Kang-Yup Na, Kenneth J. Woo, and John Horan
Fine scholars, valued friends, and lively conversation partners
With gratitude

Contents

Preface xi
Using This Book xv

Devotions

1. God Remembers Us 1
2. Christ Connects Heaven and Earth 3
3. God Can Restore Us to Life 5
4. All We Need for a Happy Life 7
5. Created to Set Forth the Glory of God 9
6. God Performs Promises 11
7. Trust the Mercy of God Alone 13
8. God Is the Fountain of Life 15
9. God's Benefits Excite Us to Praise 17
10. God Takes Special Care of the Poor 19
11. Continuing in Obedience 21
12. Divine Help Is Coming 23
13. We Are Not Exempt from Troubles 25
14. True Patience 27
15. All Blessings Flow from Reconciliation 29
16. Grace in Immeasurable Abundance 31

Contents

17. This Beautiful Theater 33
18. The Joy of Providence 35
19. Trust Lifts Us 37
20. God Helps Us in All Dangers 39
21. True Humility 41
22. Hope Is Steadfastness of Faith 43
23. Salvation Proceeds from God's Undeserved Kindness 45
24. Seeing What Is Not Yet 47
25. All Things Governed by God's Providence 49
26. Hope Arises from Despair 51
27. The Purpose of Living 53
28. Reformation of Our Whole Life 55
29. Life and Light 57
30. Walking in God's Paths 59
31. Silence 61
32. Our Savior 63
33. Consecrate Our All 65
34. Remission and Repentance 67
35. Forgetting to Notice Others 69
36. Lifelong Repentance 71
37. Helping Those in Need 73
38. Forgiveness Unlimited 75
39. Ready to Serve 77
40. Brought Down to Receive Life 79
41. Facing Death, Seeing Heaven 81
42. Hope for Pardon 83
43. Receive Christ by Faith 85
44. The Heart of God Poured Out in Love 87

Contents

45. Faith Is the Root of Good Works 89
46. God Takes the Initiative 91
47. Following the Word with Eyes Shut 93
48. Stirred to Gratitude 95
49. Blessed When We Serve 97
50. Only Believe 99
51. Wolves Within and Sheep Without 101
52. The Holy Spirit Is Known by Faith 103
53. The Face of Jesus Christ 105
54. Predestination Is Shown in Christ Alone 107
55. What Is Most Important 109
56. No Way . . . Yes, Way! 111
57. The Kingdom of God 113
58. Jesus Christ: Divinity and Humanity 115
59. New Creatures by Baptism 117
60. Knowledge of God's Will Is True Wisdom 119
61. God's Law Is to Encourage Love 121
62. Church Is Founded on Christ Alone 123
63. At the Table: God's Boundless Love 125
64. No Useless Church Members 127
65. The Most Excellent Way 129
66. The Foundation of the Gospel 131
67. To Restore Everything 133
68. A Better Hope 135
69. The Quarrel Is Resolved 137
70. God Draws Near to Us in Christ 139
71. We Give from Christ's Example 141
72. Relying on Christ Alone 143

Contents

73. Only Glory in God 145
74. God's Eternal Election 147
75. Our Highest End 149
76. Certainty of Faith 151
77. Be Whatever We Are for Others 153
78. Happy in Life and Death 155
79. Our Chief Desire 157
80. Called by God 159
81. What Is the Gospel? 161
82. The Spirit Shows Us Hidden Things 163
83. Receiving Christ in the Poor 165
84. Love Proves God Abides in Us 167

Selected Resources for Further Reflections 169

Preface

THIS BOOK IS A supplement and complement to my *Coffee with Calvin: Daily Devotions* (2013). That book presented devotional reflections based on quotations from John Calvin's major theological work, *Institutes of the Christian Religion* (1559). The idea was to explain aspects of Calvin's thought and to reflect on the importance of those thoughts for contemporary Christians in the church. The book featured eighty-four devotions.[1]

Conversations with Calvin expands Calvin devotions and focuses on comments from Calvin in his biblical commentaries. John Calvin lectured and wrote on nearly all the books in the Bible. His commentaries have been a source of interpretive understanding for Christians since the sixteenth century. In the devotions that follow, quotes from Calvin's commentaries form the basis for my reflections on what Calvin's insights can mean for us today. In these devotions, a biblical passage for the devotion is listed, which is usually the portion of Scripture from which the quotation from Calvin that is the focus of the devotion is drawn. This enables us to hear Calvin's insights on biblical texts which themselves are sources for contemplation and reflection.

1. My related books with this purpose have been *Coffee with Calvin: Daily Devotions* (Louisville: Westminster John Knox, 2013); *Moments with Martin Luther: 95 Daily Devotions* (Louisville: Westminster John Knox, 2016); *Mornings with Bonhoeffer: 100 Reflections on the Christian Life* (Nashville: Abingdon, 2018); and *Breakfast with Barth: Daily Devotions* (Eugene, OR: Cascade, 2019). Protestant Reformers were presented in *The Sanctuary for Lent 2017* (Nashville: Abingdon, 2016) and *Advent: A Calendar of Devotions* (Nashville: Abingdon, 2017).

PREFACE

Calvin's commentaries lend themselves to this type of devotional focus because Calvin wrote clearly about the key theological and practical dimensions of biblical passages. He believed it was important to understand what the biblical writer meant in the original context of a passage. He also wanted to understand what the meaning of the text was for Christians in the time in which Calvin lived. By extension, now, we listen not only to the biblical passage itself, but also to Calvin's interpretation of it as we reflect on what the biblical passage can mean for us today. Calvin was concerned with the "use" of the text for the people of God and not only the kinds of questions that are asked about the historical or cultural contexts of the biblical writings.[2] This is what Calvin meant when he wrote that "in the reading of Scripture we ought ceaselessly to endeavor to seek out and meditate upon those things which make for edification."[3] Interpreting Scripture as God's word should focus on edification, which is "the upbuilding of Christians in the Christian church and thus the strengthening of their faith and devotion to God in Jesus Christ."[4]

My hope is that with Calvin as a guide, the Scriptures will continue to speak to us in new and fresh ways. These devotions are meant to open doors to reflections on what the Scripture is saying, by the work of the Holy Spirit, and what meanings the biblical messages can have for us. They point to some specific aspects of Calvin's theology, but most of all they feature Calvin as an interpreter who listens to biblical texts and tries to understand what God is saying in and through these texts to the church of Jesus Christ. Calvin was a church theologian, recognizing Scripture as God's word which comes to us through human authors and which, by the guidance of God's Holy Spirit, can convey to us what God wants us to believe and how God wants us to live. If this book

---

2. For Calvin's views on Scripture and biblical interpretation, see McKim, "Calvin's View of Scripture," 43–68; Rogers and McKim, *Authority and Interpretation*, 89–116; and McKim, *Calvin and the Bible*. More widely on Calvin, see McKim, *Cambridge Companion to John Calvin*, and McKim, *John Calvin*.

3. Calvin, *Institutes of the Christian Religion*, 1.14.4.

4. See McKim, *Westminster Dictionary of Theological Terms*, 99.

PREFACE

of devotions can help by enabling us to listen to the Scriptures as Calvin understood them, that will be a cause for rejoicing!

Some specific suggestions for using this book follow. I hope these will enhance the book and enable it to be significant on a number of levels. The book is simply structured to follow the biblical order of the Scripture passages that are the focus of the comments quoted from Calvin. The book can be for daily use and the devotions read in whatever order one desires. John Calvin had a robust view of the providence of God and the work of God's Spirit. My theological hope is the Holy Spirit will use the devotions to bless the lives of those who read them.

As always, I deeply appreciate the help of Robin Parry of Wipf & Stock Publishers. Robin has been most supportive of this work and I am grateful to him. It is always good to work with Wipf & Stock Publishers with all the fine folks and friends on the staff. I am most appreciative of their publishing program.

My loving family shares what is most important in life with me. Their love and support mean more to me than I can ever express. My wife, LindaJo, shares life with me in wonderful ways and she means the world to me. Our son, Stephen, and his wife, Caroline, bring us joy, along with their children, Maddie, Annie, and Jack. Our son, Karl, and his wife, Lauren, bring happiness as we share life. Our family times together are precious gifts of God.

This book is dedicated to three friends. Kang-Yup Na is a longtime professor at Westminster College, New Wilmington, Pennsylvania, which is my alma mater. Kang is an insightful biblical scholar with strong theological understandings and a great appreciation for Calvin. I very much value our friendship and Kang's many ministries.

Kenneth J. Woo teaches church history at Pittsburgh Theological Seminary. He is an expert Calvin scholar and a fine teacher. Ken contributes to our understandings of John Calvin in many ways and it is a joy to talk with him about Calvin and learn from him. I am glad for Ken's ministries in scholarship and theological education and delight in our friendship.

John Horan is a friend who has carried out an oral history project for Pittsburgh Theological Seminary, called "Early Years,

Preface

Consolidating Memories." It has featured John's interviews with persons who reflect on the consolidation of Pittsburgh-Xenia and Western Theological Seminaries in 1959 to form Pittsburgh Theological Seminary. John is bright and skilled and jumped into this project, experiencing something akin to a "baptism by immersion." I am very grateful for his fine work and for hours of discussion about the two Presbyterian seminaries. It has been a joy to collaborate with John and enjoy our friendship.

My interest in John Calvin is long-standing and has been nurtured by teachers, colleagues, and friends. It stretches back to my home church pastor during my high school years, Rev. John E. Karnes. John secured my first copy of Calvin's *Institutes* for me and helped introduce me to Calvin. Dr. Jack Rogers was my beloved teacher and eventually co-author, with whom I read Calvin at Westminster College. Our work together was invaluable. Dr. Ford Lewis Battles, the incomparable Calvin scholar and my cherished teacher, shared insights at Pittsburgh Theological Seminary that stimulated and edified me. Through my years of teaching and writing, Calvin has been a constant companion—one with whom "conversations" can always be held!

I hope this book will energize John Calvin's thought in meaningful ways. For those not familiar with Calvin, I hope the book will introduce a theologian of the word of God who seeks to understand God's word for the church and for our personal lives. For experienced Calvin readers, I hope the book will strengthen their appreciation for Calvin's insights.

Donald K. McKim
Germantown, Tennessee
Eastertide 2019

Using This Book

THIS IS A BOOK of devotions or reflections on quotations from the biblical commentaries of John Calvin (1509–64). Each piece is meant to explain the meaning of the Calvin quotation and to reflect on the theological meaning of the quotation for the church and for Christian life today. The quotes are drawn from Calvin's Old and New Testament commentaries (abbreviated as CNTC). Calvin quotations without a footnote are from the Calvin passage at the top of each devotion.

Both groups and individuals can use this book. The selections are appropriate for use in various church gatherings. Individuals can use the pieces during times of reflection and devotion.

The book features a biblical passage to be used in conjunction with the devotion. The order of the devotions follows the canonical order or order in the Bible of the biblical passage.

Several elements can be helpful in using the book.

Read and Meditate on the Scripture Passage. The Scripture passage at the top of the page provides a biblical focus for the devotion. Read it, think about it, and pray about it as you begin to read the devotion.

Read the Devotion. Each piece is written compactly, so each sentence is important. The individual sentences can be a source for reflection as each one is read. After each sentence, you can pause and reflect on its meaning.

Meditate on the Quotation and Devotion. Questions relating to Calvin's quotation and the devotion that follow can help focus meditation:

Using This Book

- ❖ What is Calvin saying here?
- ❖ What does Calvin's thought mean for the life of the church?
- ❖ What does Calvin's thought mean for my own life of faith?
- ❖ What new or changed attitudes am I led toward through Calvin's thought?
- ❖ What are ways Calvin's thought can be enacted in the life of the church community and in my own life?

Pray about this Devotion. Reflect on your meditations and gather your thoughts into a prayer in which you ask God's Holy Spirit to lead you into ways God wants you to believe and live.

Act on the Insights You Receive. Decide on ways this devotion can affect your life and begin to put these ways of believing and living into your service for Christ. Reorient ways of living. Follow new directions for your Christian witness according to God's will.

++++

The title of each devotion can be a phrase to bring its key insights to mind. As you review the titles of each devotion, recall the important meanings that emerge from each piece.

If you keep a journal, you can summarize what the quotation/reflection means to you and how it can impact your life. You can periodically review these summaries in the future.

You can also consult titles from the "Selected Resources for Further Reflection" section to read more of Calvin's works and works about John Calvin.

GENESIS 7:17 — 8:5

1

God Remembers Us

> Let us therefore learn, by this example, to repose on the providence of God, even while he seems to be most forgetful of us; for at length, by affording us help, he will testify that he has been mindful of us.[1]

++++

WE HAVE TO EMPATHIZE with Noah. He was 600 years old, was commanded by God to build an ark, and gathered his family into it, along with two animals of every species. Then it started to rain. And "the waters swelled on the earth for one hundred fifty days" (Gen 7:24). Water, water, everywhere . . .

But through it all, "God remembered Noah" (8:1). While God had promised Noah and his family safety or "salvation," this was a long time to live on an ark! Calvin speculates that Noah "might infer, that his life had been prolonged, in order that he might be more miserable than any of the rest of mankind." He may have felt

---

1. *Commentary on Genesis 8:1.*

he was sailing into oblivion and that God was absent. Noah may have been sorely tempted; his faith and patience sorely tried. But Noah persevered!

"God remembered Noah." Calvin wrote that we learn from Noah's example of faith "to repose on the providence of God, even while he seems to be most forgetful of us; for at length, by affording us help, he will testify that he has been mindful of us."

Noah continued to believe God's promise. He and his family and the animals were saved when the ark came to rest on the mountains of Ararat and dry land returned. Then God gave Noah a sign of the divine promise never to destroy every living creature again: the rainbow (8:20—9:17).

We go through "deep waters" in life. Like Noah, we may feel God has abandoned us. But God remembers us! God's help comes. When it does, we know God has been "mindful of us" all the time. Faith perseveres!

Genesis 28:10–17

2

Christ Connects Heaven and Earth

It is Christ alone, therefore, who connects heaven and earth: he is the only Mediator who reaches from heaven down to earth: he is the medium through which the fullness of all celestial blessings flows down to us, and through which we, in turn, ascend to God. He it is who, being the head over angels, causes them to minister to his earthly members.[2]

++++

WE KNOW THE STORY of Jacob's ladder. Jacob was on the move and had a dream. There was a ladder "set up on the earth, the top of it reaching to heaven; and the angels of God were ascending and descending on it" (Gen 28:12).

"Jacob's ladder," with angels ascending and descending, was taken by Calvin to be a "figure of Christ" or a "symbol of Christ." It stands for Jesus Christ, said Calvin, who alone connects heaven and earth: he is the only Mediator who reaches from heaven down

2. *Commentary on Genesis 28:12.*

to earth: he is the medium through which the fullness of all celestial blessings flows down to us, and through which we, in turn, ascend to God. He it is who, being the head over angels, causes them to minister to his earthly members."

Jesus Christ is the mediator between God and humanity (Heb 8:1, 6; 9:15; 12:24). He is the one in whom "the whole fullness of deity dwells bodily" (Col 2:9; cf. 1:19). He became a human being and died on the cross to bring God and humanity together, in reconciliation. He came to us to bring us to God. Jesus brings us blessings and brings God's presence to us in our daily lives. Jesus joins us with himself and opens heaven to us. He is the one through whom our sin is forgiven. Jesus Christ is the only mediator—the one who "connects heaven and earth."

PSALM 13

3

God Can Restore Us to Life

Certainly our confidence of life depends on this, that although the world may threaten us with a thousand deaths, yet God is possessed of numberless means of restoring us to life.[3]

++++

SURELY THERE WOULD BE no worse feeling than that we have been forgotten by God. What could be more awful?

The psalmist experienced this: "How long, O LORD? Will you forget me forever? How long will you hide your face from me? How long must I bear pain in my soul, and have sorrow in my heart all day long" (Ps 13:1–2)?

The only thing to do is to pray: "Consider and answer me, O LORD my God! Give light to my eyes, or I will sleep the sleep of death" (13:3). As Calvin put it, the writer "implores the aid and succor of God, the only remedy which remained for him."

---

3. *Commentary on Psalm 13:3.*

The psalmist prayed. His hope is that God's promises to bless and help will be real for him. "Consider and answer me, O LORD my God" (13:3)! Hope continues. Trusting in God's "steadfast love" leads to the hope of rejoicing in God's salvation when God deals "bountifully with me" (13:5–6).

The psalmist's hopeful trust is in God. Said Calvin: "Certainly our confidence of life depends on this, that although the world may threaten us with a thousand deaths, yet God is possessed of numberless means of restoring us to life."

This is our hope too, is it not? Our only hope in living is that when various "deaths" surround us, as they do throughout life, we will believe God can restore us to life! God has "numberless means" of doing this, which we often forget. We want God to "restore us" in the ways we think best. But God is at work, in ways we do not know. God can and will restore life. God gives us hope and courage!

PSALM 16

4

All We Need for a Happy Life

We have sufficient cause for being contented, since he who has in himself an absolute fullness of all good has given himself to be enjoyed by us. In this way we will experience our condition to be always pleasant and comfortable; for he who has God as his portion is destitute of nothing which is requisite to constitute a happy life.[4]

++++

WHAT DO WE REALLY need to be happy in life?

For many the answer is all the "things" our culture commands are necessary: lots of money, lots of fame, lots of security. In our serious moments, we recognize these are not—ultimately—enough. We need a source of happiness that goes beyond what comes and goes for us in our "careers" and our "drive to acquire."

In Psalm 16, the psalmist prayed for the security of a good life. But he chose to trust in God: "The LORD is my chosen portion and my cup; you hold my lot" (16:5). The psalmist knew his whole

---

4. *Commentary on Psalm 16:6.*

life was surrounded by the God in whom he trusts and who holds his life secure, in every way.

He continued: "The boundary lines have fallen for me in pleasant places; I have a goodly heritage." The psalmist experienced the goodness of God in the pleasant dimensions of life, in all he had been given, and in all with which he had been blessed.

This is all we need for a happy life. Calvin commented: "We have sufficient cause for being contented, since he who has in himself an absolute fullness of all good has given himself to be enjoyed by us. In this way we will experience our condition to be always pleasant and comfortable; for he who has God as his portion is destitute of nothing which is requisite to constitute a happy life." This says it all. We enjoy God who gives the fullness of God's own self—to us! This is all we need!

PSALM 30

5

Created to Set Forth the Glory of God

> For what purpose hast thou created me, O God! but that through the whole course of my life I may be a witness and a herald of thy grace to set forth the glory of thy name?[5]

++++

In Psalm 30, the psalmist—David, for Calvin—gives thanks to God for recovery from a serious illness. God is praised for healing and bringing life (Ps 30:1–3).

In the midst of need, the psalmist cried to the Lord: "What profit is there in my death, if I go down to the Pit? Will the dust praise you? Will it tell of your faithfulness?" (30:9). His death would be of no use to God. If he were dead, he could not celebrate the praises of God. He could not tell of God's faithfulness. This was the psalmist's argument to God in prayer.

---

5. *Commentary on Psalm* 30:9.

Assumed here is that our human lives are given so we can serve God, celebrate the praises of God, and tell of God's faithfulness. Calvin commented that it were as if David had said: "For what purpose hast thou created me, O God! but that through the whole course of my life I may be a witness and a herald of thy grace to set forth the glory of thy name?" David's death would have reduced him to "eternal silence."

Calvin's interpretation of David's life is the same as for us. We too have a purpose in being created by God. Throughout our life's journey, we are to be a witness and proclaim God's grace. We are to express the glory of God's name. How's that for a life's purpose?!

Our lives are not given by God so we can wander aimlessly about. No. We have a mission; a mission to point others to God's grace as we proclaim God's grace—known to us now in Jesus Christ. In all we do, we set forth the glory of God (see 1 Cor 10:31)!

PSALM 31

6

God Performs Promises

David desires to be delivered in the righteousness of God, because God displays his righteousness in performing his promise to his servants.[6]

++++

We all make promises. Many promises. From promising to meet for a meal to promising to pay our credit card, to solemn promises made in marriage—promises are part of our lives.

We intend to keep our promises. But sadly, this doesn't always happen. We fail to keep promises. Others fail to keep their promises. Broken promises are part of life, too.

Only one person never breaks promises: God. God performs promises. God makes good on promises, without fail. God's promises are utterly dependable in a way we do not experience anywhere else in life. God does what God says God will do. We can depend on God—the One who keeps promises.

6. *Commentary on Psalm 31:1.*

The psalmist in Psalm 31 (Calvin sees him as David) prayed: "In you, O Lord, I seek refuge; do not let me ever be put to shame; in your righteousness deliver me" (31:1). Calvin commented on this: "David desires to be *delivered in the righteousness of God,* because God displays his righteousness in performing his promise to his servants." God is dependable because God is righteous. God performs promises. Calvin went on to write:

> It is easy to see from the frequent use of the term in the Psalms, that God's righteousness means his faithfulness, in the exercise of which he defends all his people who commit themselves to his guardianship and protection. David, therefore, confirms his hope from the consideration of the nature of God, who cannot deny himself, and who always continues like himself.

God is "righteous" because God is faithful. God promises to be with the people of God and this is a promise to depend on—through all life. Rejoice that God is, and always will be, the righteous God. God performs promises!

PSALM 32

7

Trust the Mercy of God Alone

The more eminently that any one excels in holiness, the farther he feels himself from perfect righteousness, and the more clearly he perceives that he can trust in nothing but the mercy of God alone.[7]

++++

Psalm 32 is a great psalm proclaiming God's forgiveness of our sin. This is our greatest happiness: "Happy are those whose transgression is forgiven, whose sin is covered" (Ps 32:1).

Forgiveness comes from God. We cannot attain it on our own. We cannot "merit" God's forgiveness for our offenses against God. We break God's laws; fail in the love to which God calls us; and our sinful actions can bring harm and heartache. We cannot remove sin's stain upon us or take away our guilt by simply deciding to do so. Only God can forgive. Only God's mercy can remove our iniquity and guilt; only God's steadfast love can forgive our transgressions.

7. *Commentary on Psalm 32:1.*

We trust in God's mercy alone. This is what the psalmist discovered. Even after forgiveness, there is no righteousness within one's self. We sin and sin again. Calvin noted that "the more eminently that any one excels in holiness, the farther he feels himself from perfect righteousness, and the more clearly he perceives that he can trust in nothing but the mercy of God alone." Through our whole lives, it is only in the mercy of God that our hope and help can be found.

Our growth in Christian faith shows us this more clearly. No matter how much we do, or how well we do it, we see ever more clearly how far short we fall of the lives God desires for us. Calvin said it does not profit us anything once we have "entered the way of righteousness, unless the same grace" which brought us into it accompanies us to "the last step" of our lives. We continually trust the mercy of God alone!

Psalm 36

8

God Is the Fountain of Life

David . . . here affirms from the experience of the godly, and as it were in their name, that the fountain of life is in God. By this he means, that there is not a drop of life to be found without him, or which flows not from his grace.[8]

++++

It is easy to fall into the habit of living life "on the surface"—going along with little thought of God or of God's activities in our lives. We can become so busy with everyday needs and plans that we try to keep things going without looking beneath the surface of our activities to recognize God is there!

But when life's busyness deflects us from recognizing God, there is an image that sets God where God deserves to be. The psalmist recounts God's great "steadfast love" (36:5, 7) and "righteousness" (36:6), and the ways God fully provides "abundance" so

---

8. *Commentary on Psalm 36:9.*

God's people can "drink from the river of your delights" (36:8). In short, God is "the fountain of life" (36:9).

Calvin wrote that "David . . . here affirms from the experience of the godly, and as it were in their name, that the fountain of life is in God. By this he means, that there is not a drop of life to be found without him, or which flows not from his grace."

Do we recognize there is not "a drop of life" found without God? Or, that no life flows to us, except from God's grace? This puts things in perspective, doesn't it? Beneath and throughout all life is God's grace. God's "steadfast love" and "righteousness" sustain us, no matter what life brings. The source of all goodness in life is the ongoing grace of God. The never-failing source of life is God's grace, providing for us. Every "drop of life" is God's gift! Recognize this. Give deepest and most joyful thanksgiving to God for loving grace, which is for us "the fountain of life!"

PSALM 71

9

God's Benefits Excite Us to Praise

> There being nothing which ought to be more effectual in kindling and exciting our hearts to sing the praises of God, than the innumerable benefits which he has bestowed upon us.[9]

++++

Praising God is one of the central activities of our lives! We live from our relationship with God and from God's protection and help for us every day.

The psalmist in Psalm 71 recognized the ongoing ways God's care had been real. He prayed for the continuing aid of God in facing his life, a life endangered by the wicked (71:4), enemies (71:10), and accusers (71:13).

But through it all, he recognized "the mighty deeds of the LORD God" (71:16). The psalmist proclaims: "My mouth will tell of your righteous acts, of your deeds of salvation all day long, though

---

9. *Commentary on Psalm 71:15.*

their number is past my knowledge" (71:15). God's salvation leads the psalmist to declare: "my lips will shout for joy when I sing praises to you; my soul also, which you have rescued" (71:23).

Calvin comments that there is nothing more powerful in "kindling and exciting our hearts to sing the praises of God, than the innumerable benefits which he has bestowed upon us." God's blessings and benefits have been countless for us—as the psalmist recognized. They lead us to singing in praise and expressing our deepest thanksgiving and gratitude. God is the source of all life and the one who protects and helps us in life. So, we praise God!

We can see the worship service as a retelling and reliving of the history of salvation. We praise and pray to the God of our salvation. Each day, we reflect on God's ongoing goodness and grace—the "innumerable benefits" God has "bestowed upon us." We are excited to praise the One who saves us and blesses us! We tell of God's mighty acts and deeds of salvation "all day long" (71:24)!

PSALM 72

10

God Takes Special Care of the Poor

> God is indeed no respecter of persons; but it is not without cause that God takes a more special care of the poor than of others, since they are most exposed to injuries and violence.[10]

++++

Old Testament Israel looked to its king to embody the will of God. The king was to reflect God's will and ways for establishing the nation as a righteous people who represented God before the world and obeyed God in their laws and practices. Psalm 72 is a prayer for guidance and support for the king with its first petition being: "Give the king your justice, O God" (Ps 72:1).

One aspect of the justice Israel's king was supposed to practice was the care of the poor. Part of the prayer is for the king to "defend the cause of the poor of the people," and to "give deliverance to the needy" (72:4). Justice took on specific form when it

---

10. *Commentary on Psalm 72:4.*

resulted in a passion for the needs of the poor to be met and for the "needy" to be delivered from the crushing realities of their lives.

Calvin commented: "God is indeed no respecter of persons; but it is not without cause that God takes a more special care of the poor than of others, since they are most exposed to injuries and violence." God's heart extends to the poor and needy. They are, among God's people, the weakest and most helpless among us. The lives of the poor matter so much to God—and, the hope is, to the king as well—that they are to be specially cared for since they are the most vulnerable persons.

God's people today still have deep concerns for the poor and needy. Vulnerable people, those "most exposed to injuries and violence," need those who will defend their cause and provide, in fullest measure, for their well-being. The poor are important in the heart of God and should be in our hearts—and actions—as well!

Psalm 80

11

Continuing in Obedience

The verse, however, may be interpreted thus: O Lord! we will continue in our obedience to thee, even when our circumstances, so far as we can perceive, are hopeless; never shall the sharpness of our calamities have the effect of driving us to apostasy from thee: and when we are restored by thy grace and power, we will magnify thy name.[11]

++++

We don't live long in the Christian life before we realize our life is not "a bed of roses!" We face afflictions, calamities, sadnesses, and all manner of difficulties. We are not exempt from the negatives of life, whatever they may be.

But our commitment to God in Christ continues, no matter what befalls us. Our afflictions can also strengthen our faith. When we experience ways God brings us through our sufferings, restoring us, and deepening our faith, we can be grateful. We can

11. *Commentary on Psalm 80:18.*

glorify God. Our difficulties can lead to praise and renewed faith and hope.

The psalmist prayed for the restoration of the nation, seeking divine favor (Ps 80:14–19): "Restore us . . ." (80:19). He prays on behalf of the nation—a hopeful prayer that can be personal for each of us today: "Then we will never turn back from you; give us life, and we will call on your name" (80:18). This is commitment to God—for all life.

Calvin interpreted the prayer as: "O Lord! we will continue in our obedience to thee, even when our circumstances, so far as we can perceive, are hopeless; never shall the sharpness of our calamities have the effect of driving us to apostasy from thee: and when we are restored by thy grace and power, we will magnify thy name."

Will we make this commitment, to live in continuing obedience through hopeless circumstances, through calamities? When we are restored by God's grace, will we magnify God's name?

PSALM 85

12

Divine Help Is Coming

Even when the Divine help seems slowest in coming it is then near at hand.[12]

++++

I well remember a sermon I heard when I was a college student. Its title was "Why Doesn't God Hurry?"

This is a question we all consider. We pray, and God answers. But sometimes those answers seem mighty slow in coming! In our culture, we are used to getting "instant results." Put your money into a machine and out drops a candy bar. Or, pay in a store and walk out with the merchandise. Even when we request services from the cable TV company or order our hamburger at the drive-through, we expect fast service!

Sometimes God answers our prayers quickly. We are led to praise and thanks almost immediately. But God doesn't work "on demand," or on our timetables. Prayers may be made through

12. *Commentary on Psalm 85:9.*

months or years while we wait for God's answer or help. So we wonder, "why doesn't God hurry?"

We will never know *why* God's answers to prayer come when they do. What we do know is that God hears and answers our prayers according to what is best for us. Calvin commented on the psalmist's faith: "Surely his salvation is at hand for those who fear him," that "even when the Divine help seems slowest in coming it is then near at hand." We do not know the ways in which God is at work, even as we wait—sometimes it seems "endlessly"—for God to answer our prayers. We are encouraged to live in hope, even when to outward appearances God does not seem to be hearing or answering our petitions. We trust and hope, truly believing that even when God seems "slow," God is always "near at hand." God is always with us, even as we wait—and wait—for God to answer our prayers. Divine help is coming!

Psalm 91

13

We Are Not Exempt from Troubles

> Believers will never be exempt from troubles and embarrassments. God does not promise them a life of ease and luxury, but deliverance from their tribulations.[13]

++++

Psalm 91 is one of the great psalms assuring believers of God's protection. Through all the most difficult and life-threatening events, God protects. Snares, deadly pestilence, terrors, warfare, destruction—all are experiences that can be endured because God delivers and covers, so ultimately "no evil shall befall you, no scourge come near your tent" (Ps 91:1–10).

Those who love God will be delivered. Says God, "I will protect those who know my name" (91:14). God loves God's people who are devoted to God. A result of this communion with God is the certainty that God answers the prayers of those in need: "When they call to me, I will answer them; I will be with them in

---

13. *Commentary on Psalm 91:15.*

trouble, I will rescue them and honor them" (91:15). Through all times of trouble God is there to rescue and save.

Calvin commented that "believers will never be exempt from troubles and embarrassments. God does not promise them a life of ease and luxury, but deliverance from their tribulations." Faith prompts prayers. In the midst of deepest difficulties, believers do not ask to be exempt from their troubles, they pray for deliverance through their troubles. This is God's promise. God is with us and will rescue us.

Troubles come to all of us. We do not believe in a "prosperity Christianity" that anticipates only "smooth sailing." As the old expression goes, "I never promised you a rose garden." The Christian life is full of afflictions and distresses. But through them all, our best blessing is that God is with us. God answers our prayers and delivers us from the tribulations we face. Some way, somehow, God sees us through! We trust God. We believe God's word to us; and we believe God saves us!

PSALM 94

14

True Patience

A true patience does not consist in presenting an obstinate resistance to evils, or in that unyielding stubbornness which passed as a virtue with the Stoics, but in a cheerful submission to God, based upon confidence in his grace.[14]

++++

Most of us find it hard to be patient. We hear it said that "patience is not one of my virtues!" To wait is difficult. To wait with a positive outlook through it all is even harder.

The ancient Stoics practiced patience because they believed that "whatever will be will be." They did not try to control events, only react to them. They believed it was better to accept everything that happened with patience because events came from the blind fate that decreed everything that happened in the world. So one was resigned to one's "fate."

14. *Commentary on Psalm 94:12.*

The psalmist spoke of the discipline or instruction or afflictions that come from God (Ps 94:12). Those who experience these are called "happy" or "blessed."

On our own, we would naturally be despondent, upset, or impatient when we experience such things. We want them to be over. We are impatient to get on with other things from God.

But through it all, we are to have patience, unlike the Stoics, who faced everything with an unfeeling resignation to blind fate. Instead, said Calvin, "A true patience does not consist in presenting an obstinate resistance to evils, or in that unyielding stubbornness which passed as a virtue with the Stoics, but in a cheerful submission to God, based upon confidence in his grace."

We do not believe in a faceless fate that grinds us down through life. We believe in a God who loves us and guides us, even through difficulties. As we endure them, we submit our wills to God. We live in confidence that God's loving grace surrounds us and leads us. This is true patience—which brings blessedness.

PSALM 103:1-5

15

All Blessings Flow from Reconciliation

> He begins with God's pardoning mercy, for reconciliation with him is the fountain from which all other blessings flow.[15]

++++

Psalm 103 celebrates—in thanksgiving—God's goodness to the psalmist: "Bless the Lord, O my soul, and all that is within me, bless his holy name. Bless the Lord, O my soul, and do not forget all his benefits" (103:1-2). God's "benefits" are all God's gracious deeds that the psalmist has experienced in fullest measure.

After praising God, the psalmist went on to recount God's gracious deeds. These include God's forgiveness, healing, redemption, and his enveloping the psalmist with steadfast love and mercy. God has forgiven our iniquities. This is first and foremost among God's benefits. As Calvin wrote, the psalmist "begins with

---

15. *Commentary on Psalm 103:3.*

God's pardoning mercy, for reconciliation with him is the fountain from which all other blessings flow."

Forgiveness is God's "freely pardoning and blotting out our sins, and receiving us into his favor," wrote Calvin. This provides a new status and relationship with God. Our lives are changed in the most basic and fundamental way when our standing before God is as one who has received God's forgiving mercy and reconciliation. This new life is the "fountain" from which all the "benefits" and blessings of God flow.

God continues to show mercy and forgive our sins. We experience this forgiveness in Jesus Christ who died and was raised to reconcile us with God and give us a new life for love and service to God in Christ.

When we think of God's benefits to us, we begin with the gift of mercy and forgiveness. All we are and all we do emerge from this basic relationship established by reconciliation. An old hymn, "Count Your Many Blessings," says, "Count your many blessings, name them one by one." When we do, we begin with the blessings of God's forgiving love; and God's reconciling grace, which blesses us all our days.

PSALM 103:1–5

16

Grace in Immeasurable Abundance

Before, behind, on all sides, above and beneath, the grace
of God presents itself to us in immeasurable abundance;
so that there is no place devoid of it.[16]

++++

When we think of God, Jesus Christ, and the Holy Spirit—words
can fail us. The witness of Scripture shows us who God is and what
God has done. Our experience of salvation, offered freely and fully
in Jesus Christ, and made real to us by the Holy Spirit is unlike
anything else we know in life. Our language tries to capture what
we know. We reach for ways to put into words the deepest realities
of our lives.

The psalmist experienced God's goodness as well as God's
deliverance when God "saved" him from disaster. The psalmist
praised and "blessed" God who "redeems your life from the Pit"

---

16. *Commentary on Psalm 103:4.*

(Ps 103:4). He was at the point of death; but was delivered from death—by God—redeemed from Sheol or "the Pit" (cf. 40:2).

How to describe this redemption, this salvation? Calvin wrote that the psalmist experienced "the incomparable grace of God" in his salvation—from its beginning throughout his life. God's grace is "incomparable"—there is nothing else like it in the whole world!

God saves and "crowns" us with "steadfast love and mercy," said the psalmist. He knew this in his own experience. God's gracious love surrounded him, meaning, said Calvin, that "before, behind, on all sides, above and beneath, the grace of God presents itself to us in immeasurable abundance; so that there is no place devoid of it."

God's grace surrounds us "in immeasurable abundance"—we cannot even imagine the abundance of God's grace! There is no place or time—anywhere, anywhen in our lives—where God's grace does not wrap around us.

What if we lived—every day and every minute—realizing God's grace is with us in "immeasurable abundance?"

Psalm 104

17

This Beautiful Theater

It is no small honor that God for our sake has so magnificently adorned the world, in order that we may not only be spectators of this beauteous theater, but also enjoy the multiplied abundance and variety of good things which are presented to us in it. Our gratitude in yielding to God the praise which is his due, is regarded by him as a singular recompense.[17]

++++

If we stop to ponder the power, wisdom, and goodness of God—it takes our breath away!

Psalm 104 celebrates God as the creator and provider for the earth and all that is in it. The psalmist begins: "Bless the Lord, O my soul. O Lord my God, you are very great. You are clothed with honor and majesty" (Ps 104:1). Then follows praises for all God has created and the works God has done throughout the earth.

17. *Commentary on Psalm 104:31.*

God creates and sustains, and this to the ongoing blessing and delight of God's people!

Our enjoyments of life come from many good things—all of them brought to us by our creator God, who lovingly tends to us throughout our days. The magnificent earth is before us, leading us to praise God and to exclaim with the psalmist: "May the glory of the LORD endure forever" (104:31). This led Calvin to proclaim:

> It is no small honor that God for our sake has so magnificently adorned the world, in order that we may not only be spectators of this beauteous theater, but also enjoy the multiplied abundance and variety of good things which are presented to us in it. Our gratitude in yielding to God the praise which is his due, is regarded by him as a singular recompense.

We enjoy all the benefits of "this beautiful theater." As God's people, we should tend the earth, preserve it, and be good stewards of God's creation. We praise the bounteous God, creator, and sustainer of all the earth!

PSALM 107

18

The Joy of Providence

The joy here mentioned arises from this, that there is nothing more calculated to increase our faith, than the knowledge of the providence of God; because, without it, we would be harassed with doubts and fears, being uncertain whether or not the world was governed by chance.[18]

++++

Thanksgiving and praise. Those are the two parts of Psalm 107 (vv. 1–32, 33–42). They are also two main parts of our Christian lives.

Thanksgiving is offered to God for deliverances from many troubles during the history of Israel. God was involved in Israel's history, sustaining the nation by "steadfast love" and "wonderful works" (107:31). Praise is given to God for God's control of nature and God's special care for the poor and needy who are raised up "out of distress" (107:41). This is joyful praise and "the upright see it and are glad" (107:42).

18. *Commentary on Psalm 107:42.*

Calvin notes God's work is seen by faith and brings "unfeigned delight." People of faith have seen and experienced God's providence—which is God's leading and guiding, God's sustaining and ruling—in history and our own lives. The wicked do not perceive these works of God. They cannot see this "clear light."

But "the joy here mentioned," said Calvin, for people of faith, "arises from this, that there is nothing more calculated to increase our faith, than the knowledge of the providence of God; because, without it, we would be harassed with doubts and fears, being uncertain whether or not the world was governed by chance."

Calvin has a robust doctrine of providence, believing it is the most practical of all doctrines. Without it, we are plagued by "doubts and fears." We are uncertain whether life is governed by chance or luck. All we can do is cast our fate to the winds!

But our faith is strengthened and we can have calm in our lives when we have confidence in the benevolent providence of our loving God. This is the joy of providence!

PSALM 112

19

Trust Lifts Us

But a sense of calamities, while it alarms and disconcerts the faithful, does not make them faint-hearted, because it does not shake their faith, by which they are rendered bold and steadfast. In a word, they are not insensible to their trials, but the confidence which they place in God enables them to rise above all the cares of the present life.[19]

++++

Life is dangerous in many ways. We may not face physical dangers like our ancestors in day-to-day existence, but we are well acquainted with calamities that can bring life caving in on us. Even the daily news can put us on edge. We know human existence on the planet is precarious. News from a physician about our health can bring danger to us in an instant.

Psalm 112 enumerates a number of blessings the righteous in Israel experienced. These cover a wide range. For facing life, it is

19. *Commentary on Psalm 112:7.*

said of the righteous that "they are not afraid of evil tidings; their hearts are firm, secure in the Lord" (Ps 107:7).

Calvin commented that "a sense of calamities, while it alarms and disconcerts the faithful, does not make them faint-hearted, because it does not shake their faith, by which they are rendered bold and steadfast. In a word, they are not insensible to their trials, but the confidence which they place in God enables them to rise above all the cares of the present life."

Faith, through it all, is the key. We can face life and its troubles with boldness and steadfastness because faith is focused on God, who can sustain us and bring us through even the worst harms that befall us. We face our trials realistically. But we rely on God. We are "secure under God's protection," wrote Calvin. Confidence in God sees us through whatever we have to face. Trust in God lifts us!

PSALM 119:161–76

20

God Helps Us in All Dangers

> I have no doubt that, in commending his life in general terms to the protection of God, he thought again and again how he was shut up on every side by innumerable deaths, from which he could not escape if God did not prove his continual deliverer. But this is an inestimable comfort to us, that God assures us that in all dangers he will be ready and prepared to help us.[20]

++++

We encounter many dangers in life. These range throughout our days, affecting us in countless ways. Some face physical dangers. For others, dangers lurk within our unconsciousness or plague us by disrupting our lives. Spiritual dangers can lure us away from following God's will toward being totally self-possessed and self-focused. Dangers can paralyze us with worries and fears.

How do we escape dangers or deal with dangers? There is only one way: by trusting God. The psalmist prayed: "Let my

---

20. *Commentary on Psalm 119:170.*

supplication come before you; deliver me according to your promise" (Ps 119:170). In prayer, we ask God to deliver us. *Only God* can save us from dangers without and within. *Only God* can deliver us from the evils that threaten us. Our only hope is to pray and trust God to rescue and liberate us from the dangers that can destroy.

Calvin commented that the psalmist was "shut up on every side by innumerable deaths, from which he could not escape if God did not prove his continual deliverer. But this is an inestimable comfort to us, that God assures us that in all dangers he will be ready and prepared to help us."

This is our only comfort, isn't it? That God promises and assures us in the midst of all the threats and jeopardies we can face that God is ready and willing to help us. This is our only hope and comfort! This is the promise we trust: God helps us in all dangers!

ISAIAH 6:1–8

21

True Humility

> Until God reveal[s] himself to us, we do not think that we are men, or rather, we think that we are gods; but when we have seen God, we then begin to feel and know what we are. Hence springs true humility, which consists in this, that a man makes no claims for himself, and depends wholly on God.[21]

++++

A dramatic Old Testament story is Isaiah's encounter with God in the temple (Isa 6:1–8). His vision was of the Lord sitting on a throne, "high and lofty" (Isa 6:1). Heavenly beings—six-winged seraphs—attended God. They called to each other: "Holy, holy, holy is the Lord of hosts; the whole earth is full of his glory." Confronted with this glorious God, Isaiah could only confess: "Woe is me! I am lost, for I am a man of unclean lips" (6:5).

Calvin sees Isaiah as "so terrified as to resemble a dead man." In the presence of the almighty God, the Lord of hosts, what else

---

21. *Commentary on Isaiah 6:5*.

could Isaiah say? His life in relation to the Supreme Creator of all, the glorious Lord, was limited and finite . . . and sinful. He had transgressed God's law, broken God's commandments, and fallen short of the life God wanted Isaiah to live. He had "unclean lips" in the midst of an unclean community.

On his own, Isaiah—or we—might think "we are gods," said Calvin. But "when we have seen God, we then begin to feel and know what we are." Our perspective is set right: God is God, and we are not. We see ourselves in relation to the holy God and we realize our own unholiness.

"Hence springs true humility," said Calvin, "which consists in this, that a man makes no claims for himself, and depends wholly on God." This true humility is our only hope—recognizing the reality of our limits and sins before God. So, we must depend wholly on God. No self-claims to goodness or virtue; only casting ourselves fully on the Lord in true humility.

ISAIAH 30:18-22

22

Hope Is Steadfastness of Faith

> He enjoins them to "wait," that is, to hope. Now, hope is nothing else than steadfastness of faith, that is, when we wait calmly till the Lord fulfill what he has promised. . . . Without hope in God there can be no salvation or happiness.[22]

++++

In the midst of Israel's oppression by Assyria, a prophetic word for the future burst forth! God promised Zion: "Therefore the LORD waits to be gracious to you; therefore he will rise up to show mercy to you. For the LORD is a God of justice; blessed are all those who wait for him" (Isa 30:18).

This word came to people who felt hopeless. Alliances with other countries, such as Egypt, would not save the people. They could only hope for God's kindness and aid.

The prophetic word promised God would be gracious to the people and would show mercy. In their waiting, they hoped. They

---

22. *Commentary on Isaiah 30:18.*

were to live by faith in anticipation of God's fulfilling the divine promise. As Calvin put it, God "enjoins them to 'wait,' that is, to hope. Now, hope is nothing else than steadfastness of faith, that is, when we wait calmly till the Lord fulfill what he has promised. . . . Without hope in God there can be no salvation or happiness."

Our situation today is vastly different from the people of Israel. But we are also a people of God who wait in anticipation for the future and for salvation. The coming reign of God over all the earth is God's ultimate purpose. Today, we wait, calmly, in hopeful anticipation of the fulfillment of this coming world of promise. Our waiting is our hope—our faith—holding steady as history progresses and our own lives develop. In the midst of the difficulties we face—and disappointments all around us—hope is steadfastness of faith. Without hope in God, "there can be no salvation or happiness," said Calvin. We hope as we live in faith!

ISAIAH 49:8-12

23

Salvation Proceeds from God's Undeserved Kindness

> Our salvation proceeds from God's undeserved kindness. [Heb.] *Ratzon* which the Greeks translate εὐδοκία (*eudokia*), that is, the good-will of God is the foundation of our salvation; and salvation is the effect of that grace. We are saved, because we please God, not through our worthiness or merits, but by his free grace.[23]

++++

The people of Israel were exiled in Babylon. This was devastating. Their homeland was in ruins and they were forced to live in a land where the God of Israel was not worshiped. Year after year, the people sought deliverance from God and a return to the land God had given them.

---

23. *Commentary on Isaiah 49:8.*

The voice of the prophet, identified as Isaiah, came to the people with God's promise that they would be brought home by God's power. This was deliverance, liberation, salvation!

Calvin applied this promise of salvation for Israel to the salvation of God's people now, who have been chosen by God and saved by God's good will—grace—and kindness. Calvin wrote: "Our salvation proceeds from God's undeserved kindness. [Heb.] *Ratzon* which the Greeks translate εὐδοκία (*eudokia*), that is, the good-will of God is the foundation of our salvation; and salvation is the effect of that grace. We are saved, because we please God, not through our worthiness or merits, but by his free grace."

For Christians, salvation is by God's grace in Jesus Christ. We have been chosen by God in Christ, who died for our salvation and the forgiveness of our sins. Jesus is God's grace "in person." God sent Christ in gracious love, expressing "undeserved kindness" (Calvin) to us and God's good will. This is the foundation of our salvation, as Calvin says. Not by merit or goodness on our part are we saved, but by God's free grace. No greater gift can be given to us! Praise the God of our salvation!

ISAIAH 52:1-12

24

Seeing What Is Not Yet

> But in the promises of God, as in a mirror, we ought to
> behold those things which are not yet visible to our eyes,
> even though they appear to us to be contrary to reason.[24]

++++

God's promise to restore the people of Israel to their homeland from their exile in Babylon brought rejoicing: "Break forth together into singing, you ruins of Jerusalem; for the LORD has comforted his people, he has redeemed Jerusalem" (Isa 52:9).

Against all odds, God's promise was made—and would be fulfilled. This is the sure promise, received in faith by God's people awaiting their deliverance and salvation.

This is the nature of faith, isn't it? Faith is, as the writer of Hebrews said, "the assurance of things hoped for, the conviction of things not seen" (Heb 11:1). Faith is an assurance—based on God's promise, for that for which we hope—a deep belief in "things not

---

[24]. *Commentary on Isaiah 52:9.*

seen." For Paul, "we walk by faith, not by sight" (2 Cor 5:7). We see beyond the present and the apparent to that which God has promised, which is not yet seen.

Calvin commented on the Isaiah passage: "But in the promises of God, as in a mirror, we ought to behold those things which are not yet visible to our eyes, even though they appear to us to be contrary to reason." By faith we trust in God's promises "not yet visible to us." Even when God's promises appear to be "contrary to reason" we continue to trust and believe. If God's promises were nothing more than a magnification of our own powers of reasoning we could not depend on them, could we? Just because we can "reason" it, there is no guarantee something will become so. But God's promises, received in faith, are trustworthy and will be fulfilled, because they come from God. We trust God's word, not our reasoning powers. Faith is seeing what is not yet. Look ahead in faith!

JEREMIAH 10:23-25

25

All Things Governed by God's Providence

For what men commonly call fortune is nothing else but God's providence. Since then God by his hidden counsel governs the affairs of men, it follows that all events prosperous or adverse, are at his will. Whatever, then, men may consult, determine, and attempt, they yet can execute nothing, for God gives such an issue as he pleases.[25]

++++

Calvin had a comprehensive view of God's providence. Anchored in Scripture, Calvin believed the doctrine of providence expressed God's nature. God is an active, involved God. God acts in history and in the lives of human beings, sustaining, cooperating, and guiding events and people.

Providence is also a crucially necessary doctrine for Christian living. We are aware of God's involvement with us. God sustains

25. *Commentary on Jeremiah 10:23.*

us, day by day. God cooperates with us so we can do God's will. God guides us in carrying out God's purposes so we may live to God's glory.

We are not left to deal with life as a series of "fortunes" or "misfortunes." We are not cast about on waves of danger and uncertainty. God is at work within us and among us, carrying out God's "hidden counsel," said Calvin, governing our activities and the events of our lives. For Calvin, this means that events "prosperous or adverse" are all at God's will. In the difficulties of life, whatever they may be, we can be assured that God is there, leading and guiding, helping and sustaining us.

Our own actions and plans, whatever they may be, find their results in God's purposes and plan. This gives us incredible freedom to launch out in faith with actions, trusting God to bless and help according to God's will. We launch out, believing, in faith. The prophet Jeremiah knew that "the way of human beings" is in God's control, not ours. God directs our steps (Jer 10:23). This is not blind fate. God is the God who loves us with a parental love. We trust and entrust ourselves to God, in all things!

LAMENTATIONS 3:16–24

26

Hope Arises from Despair

> He who is conscious of his own infirmity, and directs his prayer to God, will at length find a ground of hope. . . . A sense of our own infirmity draws us even close to him; thus hope, contrary to nature, and through the incomprehensible and wonderful kindness of God, arises from despair.[26]

++++

The book of Lamentations is well named. In devastating circumstances, the writer "laments" with deep feelings of infirmity and despair. Afflictions abound, even a sense that God has rejected the writer: "I am one who has seen affliction under the rod of God's wrath" (Lam 3:1).

In graphic language, the despair breaks forth: "The thought of my affliction and my homelessness is wormwood and gall! My soul continually thinks of it and is bowed down within me" (3:19–20). Then something changes: "But this I call to mind and therefore

---

26. *Commentary on Lamentations 3:21.*

I have hope: The steadfast love of the LORD never ceases" (3:22). Recognition of the infirmity and need one faces turns one away from one's self and directs us to pray to God.

Calvin commented that "a sense of our own infirmity draws us even close to him; thus hope, contrary to nature, and through the incomprehensible and wonderful kindness of God, arises from despair." It is when we are at "the end of our rope," when our despair is nearly total, then we are able to be drawn close to God. We do not trust in ourselves; we can trust only in God. Our despair and infirmity themselves are our cause of hope. This is contrary to what we expect—we think we should be able to pull ourselves up and out of our situations. But we can't. We'd like to think we are self-sufficient and self-secure. But we aren't.

We experience "the incomprehensible and wonderful kindness of God," which arises from despair. We trust God and remember God's "steadfast love never ceases." This is the word of hope which saves. Hope arises from despair!

DANIEL 3:16-18

27

The Purpose of Living

> For of what use is life except to serve God's glory? But we lose that object in life for the sake of the life itself—that is, by desiring to live entirely to the world, we lose the very purpose of living![27]

++++

When the four young Israelites at the Babylonian court would not bow down and worship the golden statue that King Nebuchadnezzar had set up, the king went into a "furious rage" (Dan 3:13). He asked: "Is it true, O Shadrach, Meshach, and Abednego, that you do not serve my gods and you do not worship the golden statue that I have set up" (3:14)? The Israelites faced being thrown into a fiery furnace for this disobedience. But they trusted God to deliver them. They said, "We will not serve your gods and we will not worship the golden statue that you have set up" (3:18). Then the God of Israel delivered the Israelites from the fiery furnace.

---

27. *Commentary on Daniel 3:18.*

The three Israelites were obedient to their faith. They would only worship God, giving God the worship and praise due to the Lord. They would not capitulate to their surrounding culture or be drawn into worshiping false gods.

Calvin notes that in doing this, the three Israelites were upholding their purpose for living. The same is true for us. Calvin wrote: "For of what use is life except to serve God's glory? but we lose that object in life for the sake of the life itself—that is, by desiring to live entirely to the world, we lose the very purpose of living!" Our life's purpose is to live for the glory of God. But when we lose sight of that purpose and desire to live "entirely to the world"—adopting its values and living without thought of God— we lose "the very purpose of living." Seeking what the world gives and worshiping "statues" that the world erects turns us away from true life—worshiping and serving God. Live out your purpose for living!

HOSEA 12:1–6

28

Reformation of Our Whole Life

Repentance is nothing else but a reformation of the whole life according to the law of God. For God has explained his will in his law; and as much as we depart or deviate from it, so much we depart from the Lord.[28]

++++

The prophet Hosea had a deep concern. His message was that the relationship between God and Israel was in danger. All through Israel's history, God had been faithful, but God's chosen people had been unfaithful. This expressed itself in apostasy, accepting other gods, not truly worshiping or serving *the* God. Other sins followed in worship, politics, and the social life.

Hosea preached for the people to repent: "But as for you, return to your God, hold fast to love and justice, and wait continually for your God" (Hos 12:6). Returning to God means repenting, turning from sin, and living into God's will and way. Calvin wrote:

---

28. *Commentary on Hosea 12:6.*

"Repentance is nothing else but a reformation of the whole life according to the law of God. For God has explained his will in his law; and as much as we depart or deviate from it, so much we depart from the Lord."

Repentance embraces our whole lives, every aspect. There are no areas exempt from the need to have them conform with God's will. God's will is known through the law of God. Calvin always emphasized this and it is important for us today. If we want to know what God desires—look at the law of God. Even further, look to Jesus Christ, who interpreted and fulfilled the law. To depart from God's law is to sin and be separated from the Lord.

Calvin went on to say that when we repent and our life is reformed, we worship God rightly and "we act kindly and justly towards our neighbors, and abstain from all injuries, frauds, robberies, and all kinds of wickedness. This is the true evidence of repentance."

May our whole lives be reformed by repentance!

JOEL 2:30–32

29

Life and Light

God offers life to us in death, and light in the darkest grave.[29]

++++

The prophet Joel anticipated a time when God's Spirit would be poured out "on all flesh" (Joel 2:28). This will occur before the "great and terrible day of the Lord comes" (2:31). Then, "everyone who calls on the name of the Lord shall be saved" (2:32).

Calvin saw this as a "remarkable passage" since "God declares that the invocation of his name in a despairing condition is a sure port of safety." Those whose hearts flee to God and who call on God's name will find safety and salvation from God's coming judgments when all places will be "filled with darkness" and judgment will be rendered.

But God reaches to those "who seem to be even in despair, and from whom God seems to have taken away every hope of

29. *Commentary on Joel* 2:32.

grace, provided they call on the name of God, will be saved, as the Prophet declares, though they be in so great a despair, and in so deep an abyss." This is the power of God, expressed in even the most hopeless situation. Calvin said, "we see how efficacious the promise is; for God offers life to us in death, and light in the darkest grave."

Life in death and light in the darkest grave. This promise extends to those who experience God's power, even today. We need "life" and "light." God can give these to us—for our present lives and for our eternal future. Even in our most hopeless situations, that seem like "death," God can save by giving new life. Even in our most feared situations that seem like the "darkest grave," God can give light to bring us through all we face. We need God's life and God's light every day and into our futures.

Micah 4:1–5

30

Walking in God's Paths

> The truth of God is not, as they say, speculative, but full of energizing power. God then not only speaks to the end that every one may acknowledge that to be true which proceeds from him, but at the same time he demands obedience.... Men really profit under the teaching of God, when they form their life according to his doctrine, and be prepared with their feet to walk, and to follow whithersoever be may call them.[30]

++++

Micah 4 is a great chapter of eschatological expectation. It is the wonderful vision of the coming reign of God on earth: "In the days to come . . ." promises God through the prophet. The promise is of peace and salvation. Life is totally transformed for nations and individuals and God's reign and rule are fully established.

In the coming days, God's will and ways will be enacted. Then God will "teach us his ways" and "we may walk in his paths" (Mic

---

30. *Commentary on Micah 4:2.*

4:2). God instructs people in God's truth, teaching them God's ways.

This is so people may walk in God's paths. Calvin comments that "the truth of God is not, as they say, speculative, but full of energizing power. God then not only speaks to the end that every one may acknowledge that to be true which proceeds from him, but at the same time he demands obedience." Knowledge alone is not enough. The knowledge of God's truth must lead to the living of God's truth. This is the "energizing power" of God's ways!

God's will for the future is also God's will for the present: we "really profit under the teaching of God" when we form our lives according to God's "doctrine" or teaching. What we believe shows us how to live. God's Spirit energizes us to live God's truth. Then, too, we must be prepared with our "feet to walk" and follow wherever God calls us!

ZECHARIAH 2:6-13

31

Silence

Silence, then, is what especially belongs to the elect and the faithful; for they willingly close their mouth to hear God speaking.[31]

++++

We live in a noisy world. Sounds, sounds—all around us. We contribute to the noise. We talk. We watch TV. We use our electronic devices. Noise . . . all around! So silence may in fact be rare. The "sounds of silence" are not ones that surround us.

The prophet Zechariah, in a series of visions, sees activities between heaven and earth, a world that is in motion, and a universal perspective of God's actions, especially to restore Judah. In an interlude after the third vision (Zech 2:6–13), the prophet says, "Be silent, all people, before the LORD; for he has roused himself from his holy dwelling" (2:13).

[31]. *Commentary on Zechariah 2:13*.

Silence. Calvin comments that "by silence we are to understand, as elsewhere observed, submission." Before almighty God, silence means recognizing who God is—the sovereign Lord. Silence is "what especially belongs to the elect and the faithful; for they willingly close their mouth to hear God speaking."

This dramatic word speaks to us as well. Do we stand in silence before the Lord of the universe? Do we stop our talking to listen—to listen God's word to us? This is what is most important for us, isn't it? To hear God's word in its fullness and to hear what God says to us, to the world, to the church? What could be more imperative and vital and essential than that? We hear when we are in silence before God's word.

We stand in submissive silence to hear God's word and be ready to obey God's word. We hear God's call, God's commands, God's cry to us to live in God's ways and be the people God intends us to be.

"Be silent, all people, before the Lord." We stop our talking, tune out the noise, and listen to the Lord . . . in silence.

MATTHEW 1:18-25

32

Our Savior

Christ is not recognized, then, as truly our Saviour, until we learn to embrace by faith the free remission of sins and know that we are counted righteous before God, as men cleared of our guilt.[32]

++++

Before Joseph and Mary came together, the Lord appeared to Joseph in a dream. He was told to take Mary as his wife and that she would conceive a child "from the Holy Spirit" (Matt 1:20). He was to be named Jesus, "for he will save his people from their sins" (1:21).

This amazing news proclaimed the world's greatest message: Jesus saves! The world was in need of this message. We are all in need of this message.

When Calvin discussed this verse, he mentioned a number of images for Jesus the Savior, who saves us from "the corruption and

---

32. *Commentary on Matthew 1:23*. CNTC 1:64.

depravity of our nature" in which we are "slaves to sin, and robbed of true righteousness." Christ delivers, gives grace, liberates, expiates, and pardons us, and removes our "fatal guilt and reconciles us with God." These are ways of trying to express the mysterious and amazing work of Jesus Christ to bring salvation and new life to the world.

Calvin wrote that "Christ is not recognized, then, as truly our Saviour, until we learn to embrace by faith the free remission of sins and know that we are counted righteous before God, as men cleared of our guilt." Put another way, we can say that it is not enough to say Jesus Christ is *"a* savior," or *"the* Savior," we must be able to say, "Jesus Christ is *my* savior." We must personally appropriate the work of Christ for ourselves, confessing by faith that Christ died for me.

Through Jesus Christ we are "counted righteous before God." We receive this gift by God's grace, through faith. Our Savior changes our life! We are forgiven and our guilt is gone!

Matthew 2:1-12

33

Consecrate Our All

> Our duty is to worship Him in spirit. This is our proper and reasonable service, which He demands, that we should consecrate to Him first ourselves, then our all.[33]

++++

Part of our Christmastime experience in the church includes the story of the magi who searched for Jesus and found him (Matt 2:1–12). Sometimes called "the story of the three wise men," this incident following the birth of Jesus points to Christ as coming for the whole world—even non-Jews like these "wise men from the East" (2:1).

The "wise men" came bearing gifts for the Christ child. They believed he had "been born King of the Jews" and came "to pay him homage" (2:2). When they found Jesus they "knelt down and paid him homage. Then, opening their treasure chests they offered him gifts of gold, frankincense, and myrrh" (2:11).

---

[33]. *Commentary on Matthew 2:11*. CNTC 1:88.

These strangers gave gifts fit for a king, though Jesus was a newborn baby. Their presents were the best they could bring. They brought gifts and knelt in worship.

The wise men are models for us. Calvin wrote that "our duty is to worship Him in spirit. This is our proper and reasonable service, which He demands, that we should consecrate to Him first ourselves, then our all." We worship Jesus Christ, consecrating or dedicating ourselves to Christ; and then giving him the whole of our lives and what we have in dedicated service to following Jesus.

Worship . . . consecrating . . . serving. This is where our experience of Jesus Christ leads us. Worshiping Christ makes radical changes in our lives. We acknowledge Jesus Christ for who he is. Then our lives are committed to Jesus as our Lord and Savior. We are no longer our own, we belong to Jesus Christ (Rom 1:6). We give Christ "our all"—the complete devotion of ourselves and all we possess as "servants of Christ" (1 Cor 4:1)—to be Jesus' disciples.

Matthew 3:1–12

34

Remission and Repentance

The whole Gospel stands on two parts, Remission of sins, and Repentance.[34]

++++

By all measures, John the Baptist was a strange character! Living in the wilderness, wearing a wardrobe of "camel's hair with a leather belt around his waist," and subsisting on a diet of "locusts and wild honey," John was a fiery preacher (Matt 3:1–4). His message proclaimed "a baptism of repentance for the forgiveness of sins" (Luke 3:3; Mark 1:4): "Repent, for the kingdom of heaven has come near" (Matt 3:2). He baptized those who responded to his proclamation.

Repentance and remission (forgiveness) of sins are linked together. They are the main components of John's message, which became the Christian message. Calvin wrote that "the whole Gospel stands on two parts, Remission of sins, and Repentance."

---

34. *Commentary on Matthew 3:2.* CNTC 1:115.

To "repent" means to be sorrowful for sin and to turn around and walk in a new direction in life. In Israel, to repent meant to forsake sin and live in new ways. Calvin wanted to be clear that repentance itself is not the cause of God's forgiveness. Repentance does not induce God to forgive us or to have mercy on us in forgiveness.

Instead, repentance—walking in new ways—is the response to God's mercy by those whose sin is forgiven. God forgives and those who know God's forgiveness respond by amending and changing their lives to live as God desires. Calvin wrote that in the Scriptures, people are told to repent so "they may perceive the reconciliation that is offered to them"—especially the "free love of God" and pardon for sin. Baptism was a sign of this forgiveness. John said: "Bear fruit worthy of repentance" (Matt 3:8) and gave examples of actions in this new life (Luke 3:10–14).

For us, remission and repentance are central as well. We confess our sin and repent—turn around—and walk in new ways of obedience. Will we?

Matthew 7:7-11

35

Forgetting to Notice Others

> Christ contrasts the malice of men with the unbounded goodness of God. It is φιλαυτία (self-love; [*philautia*]) that makes us evil, for when a man gets too fond of himself, he forgets to notice other people.[35]

++++

We all remember the childhood chant: "Me first!" We ourselves have probably even said it!

This is a natural tendency of children—and adults. We look first toward what we want, our own interests, loving ourselves and seeking our desires.

Theologically, this is the human condition, the situation of sin which cuts us off from God and how God wants us to live, which is in community and love for others. When self-interest and self-love are our dominant impulses, we are "evil," as Calvin says. Luther had an image for sin: *in curvatus in se* (Latin). Humans

---

35. *Commentary on Matthew 7:8*. CNTC 1:230.

are "turned in upon themselves." Another way to put it is that we spend life looking in a mirror—at ourselves—rather than looking out a window—seeing others, seeing God.

We get a glimpse of loving others in our families when, as Jesus said, "you who are evil, know how to give good gifts to your children" (Matt 7:11). "How much more," will the good God give "good things" to those who ask? Christ "contrasts the malice of men with the unbounded goodness of God," said Calvin.

Calvin points to the Greek word *philautia* (self-love), used in 2 Timothy 3:2 and translated "lovers of themselves" to say that when we get too "fond" of ourselves, we forget "to notice other people." Who of us can say this is not us? When we are so set on our own agendas that we overlook the needs of others, we are lovers of ourselves, more than lovers of others—or of God.

From self-love to love of others. This is the movement God desires and God can create within us in Jesus Christ.

MATTHEW 11:20–24

36

Lifelong Repentance

> We know that penitence is not demanded of believers for a few days only, but that they shall zealously occupy themselves in practicing it to their life's end.[36]

++++

The phrase "sackcloth and ashes" denotes an ancient practice in which a person wore a garment and sat in ashes as a sign of mourning, especially sorrow over one's sins. This practice would go on for some time, but eventually the person would return to a "normal" existence.

In Israel, "sackcloth and ashes" were symbols of repentance, of the deep sorrow that sin produced in the heart of the sinner. Jesus made reference to this when he spoke about the repentance that should have been features of life in Bethsaida (Matt 11:20–21). Jesus was speaking of this common practice but was also pointing to a theological reality that transcended the symbolic practice.

---

36. *Commentary on Matthew 11:21.* CNTC 11:16.

Calvin wrote: "We know that penitence is not demanded of believers for a few days only, but that they shall zealously occupy themselves in practicing it to their life's end." In other words, for followers of Jesus, "repentance"—which includes sorrow for sin and walking in a new direction in life that rejects this sin in the future—is a lifelong action. Lifelong repentance is required of Jesus' disciples, not a short, symbolic activity.

We should not think of repentance as an "automatic" process. Since sin can ensnare us on a regular basis—even the same sins in our lives—we must make repentance a conscious, ongoing process. We continue to reject sin and turn away from all activities and practices that turn us away from God's will for our lives. This continues to engage us in decision-making, discerning God's purposes for us, and following in discipleship as we serve Jesus Christ.

Repentance is not a one-time event at a point in time. It is an ongoing practice that involves us in zealous obedience to God, every day—to our life's end!

MATTHEW 12:9–13

37

Helping Those in Need

But those who do not trouble to help the needy are little different from murderers.[37]

++++

Jesus was frequently in trouble with the religious leaders of his day. They believed he was not obedient to the Jewish law, especially in what it taught about what was lawful to do on the Sabbath day.

When Jesus met a man with a withered hand on the Sabbath, he was challenged by leaders on whether it was lawful to heal on the Sabbath. Jesus' response was to say that if one of the leaders had a sheep that fell into a pit on the Sabbath day, the owner would pick it up and lift it out of the pit. If so, then "how much more valuable is a human being than a sheep" (Matt 12:12)! So, said Jesus, "it is lawful to do good on the Sabbath." Then he healed the man with the withered hand.

37. *Commentary on Matthew 12:11.* CNTC 2:32.

Humans are more than beasts, so they should be helped. Along with accounts of this story in Mark (3:1–5) and Luke (6:6–10), Calvin says we are to recognize that "those who do not trouble to help the needy are little different than murderers." If one uses "Sabbath rest" as a pretext not to stand against evil and to do what God wills, then one is like a murderer.

Our own contexts differ from those of Jesus' time, but the driving impulse here is still the same: to neglect to help those in need is to do them harm. When we adhere to a "rule" rather than to the overall love Jesus calls us to show to all persons, we are actually inflicting harm on another person. By failing to meet their need, we are acting against the will and the way of Jesus.

We are called to help those in need without exception. We cannot do anything less!

MATTHEW 18:21–22

38

Forgiveness Unlimited

> He expressly declares that no limit should be set to forgiving. It is not that He intends to lay down some definite number, but rather to enjoin us never to give up.[38]

++++

One of the hardest commands Jesus gave was given to Peter. Peter asked Jesus how many times he had to forgive someone who sinned against him. Perhaps trying to show he was a generous person, Peter suggested, "As many as seven times?" Peter may have thought that's a lot! But Jesus' response must have deflated his balloon. Jesus said, "Not seven times, but, I tell you, seventy-seven times" (Matt 18:21–22; some versions say "seventy times seven").

The actual number of times for forgiveness is not the primary point here. Calvin's interpretation is that Jesus "expressly declares that no limit should be set to forgiving. It is not that He intends to

---

38. *Commentary on Matthew 18:21.* CNTC 2:234.

lay down some definite number, but rather to enjoin us never to give up."

Imagine . . . forgiveness unlimited! Can we believe it? Can we practice it?

As Calvin continued, "we must be ready to forgive not just once or twice but as often as a sinner comes to himself." In other words, as often as someone asks us to forgive them, we must forgive them.

We would want this for ourselves, wouldn't we? If we sinned against someone and asked the person to forgive us, we wouldn't want to hear: "Sorry, I can't forgive you. I've already reached my forgiveness quota!"

But even more, we offer forgiveness unlimited because this is what we receive from God. Paul said Jesus' disciples should be "forgiving one another, as God in Christ has forgiven you" (Eph 4:32). We forgive because we have been forgiven. We sin over and over, but God's love in Jesus Christ mercifully embraces us in forgiveness. Now we never give up on others, and we offer them unlimited forgiveness.

Luke 1:26–38

39

Ready to Serve

Faith establishes us before God, that we may stand in readiness to serve.[39]

++++

Mary, the mother of Jesus, has always been a model of faith. She received the miraculous word that she would be the mother of Jesus, who would be called "the Son of the Most High" and would "reign over the house of Jacob forever" (Luke 1:31–32). When she was told this would happen, even though it seemed "impossible" to her, she was told by the angel: "For nothing will be impossible with God" (1:37). This led to Mary's response: "Here I am, the servant of the Lord; let it be with me according to your word" (1:38).

This didn't mean Mary stopped having questions, or even doubts. She was a real human being, with all the same emotions and fears we would have. But Mary responded to this word to her by faith: "Let it be with me according to your word." This expressed

39. *Commentary on Luke 1:38*. CNTC 1:30.

her faith: "Here I am, the servant of the Lord." As Calvin put it, "Faith establishes us before God, that we may stand in readiness to serve."

Mary's faith is our faith as well. We too are servants of the Lord. We stand ready to serve, in whatever ways God wants to use us. Our service will not be the same as Mary's. But however we serve God throughout our lives, we do so from the posture and commitment of faith. We believe in God and we trust God. In this, Mary—and we—echo the commitment of Isaiah, who responded to God: "Here am I; send me" (Isa 6:8)!

Are we ready to serve? Are we committed to following God's will and way for us, no matter where they lead or what they entail for us? Will we make sacrifices? Will we stand for God's ways in the midst of cultural challenges and political controversies?

Daily, let us commit, in faith: "Here am I, the servant of the Lord."

Lord, help us keep the faith as we make decisions about one of your great missions, OHS. Please lead us where you need us, regardless of the challenges.

Amen

LUKE 5:1-11

40

Brought Down to Receive Life

++++

The Lord brings His people down into the grave, that He may then give them life.[40]

When Jesus commanded Peter and his friends to take their boat out to deeper waters, Peter objected. He and his partners had "worked all night long but ha[d] caught nothing." But Peter obeyed Jesus' word. The result was that "they caught so many fish that their nets were beginning to break" (Luke 5:5-6).

Peter realized he was in the presence of the Lord. His response was to fall to his knees and say, "Go away from me, Lord, for I am a sinful man!" Calvin says Peter was "alarmed at the presence of God." This was terrifying! There could be no confidence or pride here. Peter experienced a divine action in this man, Jesus; and he knew he was a sinner in Jesus' presence.

40. *Commentary on Luke 5:8.* CNTC 1:157.

But Jesus reassured him and said, "Do not be afraid" (5:10) and Peter, with his partners, "left everything and followed him" (5:11).

Calvin commented that "the Lord brings His people down into the grave, that He may then give them life." Peter confessed his sin. But "Christ puts fresh heart into Peter." From the "grave" to "discipleship"—that was Peter's experience. He was brought down under the weight of sin, but received life from Jesus' redeeming word.

We know this too. Sometimes our lives are brought "lower than low" because of our sin or circumstances. We feel hopeless and cannot help ourselves. But from this "grave" God lifts us up—unexpectedly and in ways we can't imagine—to bring us brand new life!

Jesus himself was "crucified, dead, and buried." But "on the third day he rose again from the dead" (Apostles' Creed). From death to resurrection. God can do the same for us. No matter how deep our sin or how far we have fallen, God can raise us up and give us life!

LUKE 12:49–53

41

Facing Death, Seeing Heaven

It is not natural for a man to face death, or any decline in our present state, but when we see the glory of heaven on the further shore, and the blessed and eternal peace, our longing for them shall make us face death with patience and carry us on eagerly, wherever faith and hope lead on.[41]

++++

In Jesus' last days, he said, "I have a baptism with which to be baptized, and what stress I am under until it is completed" (Luke 12:50)! Jesus was referring to his coming death, a "metaphorical baptism." The pressures were great and Jesus mentioned the stress he was under until this was completed. This was all-consuming for Jesus and while he was entering into this path freely, it was pressing upon him and he was feeling its distress.

In his words, we see the real humanity of Jesus, the ways he was facing life in this difficult time. He was confronting life—and

---

41. *Commentary on Luke 12:50.* CNTC 3:109.

his death—fully and completely. This was dramatically seen in his prayer on the eve of his crucifixion: "He prayed more earnestly, and his sweat became like great drops of blood" (Luke 22:44).

Since Jesus underwent death by crucifixion and, theologically, died for our sins (Rom 5:8), we can face our deaths, fully and completely. We do not have the weight of the world's sins upon us, as did Jesus. But Jesus' crucifixion led to his resurrection! His death and resurrection bring us eternal life, a life to anticipate in the fullness and eternal presence of God. As Calvin wrote, "It is not natural for a man to face death, or any decline in our present state, but when we see the glory of heaven on the further shore, and the blessed and eternal peace, our longing for them shall make us face death with patience and carry us on eagerly, wherever faith and hope lead on." We can face death with patience; and anticipate the glory of heaven!

LUKE 15:11–31

42

Hope for Pardon

But there is no doubt that under this image there is depicted the infinite goodness, the incomparable kindness of God, so that not the most atrocious crime need deter us from hoping for pardon.[42]

++++

One of Jesus' most well-known parables is the parable of the prodigal son (Luke 15:11–31). A preacher once made three points about the parable. The younger son was: sick at home; homesick; and home.

The son took his part of the inheritance—before his father died! He went to a "distant country," "squandered his property in dissolute living," and hit rock bottom when he ended up feeding pigs. Then he "came to himself," realized what he had done—and lost—and resolved to go home to his father, confessing his sins.

42. *Commentary on Luke 15:12*. CNTC 2:221.

Calvin commented that "sinning so much, he deserved to find his father unforgiving." This would be a natural reaction. But this was his *father*. This was his *father*, whose care for his prodigal child gushed forth from the hidden depths of his being. He ran to meet his son; and welcomed him home, in love: "he was lost and is found!" proclaimed the father.

For Calvin, "there is no doubt that under this image there is depicted the infinite goodness, the incomparable kindness of God, so that not [even] the most atrocious crime need deter us from hoping for pardon." The heart of God is a heart of overflowing love—even for hopeless sinners. God is "infinite goodness" and incomparably "kind." This love includes those who may have committed "the most atrocious crime." *Even they* have hope for pardon.

We are moved by this parable since while we can envision an earthly parent lovingly forgiving a child. *How much more* will God, whose "infinite goodness" surpasses the love of all human parents, forgive and receive us?! Our hope for pardon is with the God who receives and restores us, in our atrociousness and sinfulness, embracing us in love!

JOHN 1:1–18

43

Receive Christ by Faith

Christ offers Himself to us through the Gospel and we receive Him by faith.[43]

++++

The story of Jesus of Nazareth circulated orally throughout communities in the period after his death and resurrection. Writings that later became part of the New Testament circulated as well, including what became known as the four Gospels: Matthew, Mark, Luke, and John.

The message of Jesus Christ was written but also proclaimed orally, in preaching. The apostle Paul wrote, "So faith comes from what is heard, and what is heard comes through the word of Christ" (Rom 10:17). The faith in Christ which comes through preaching is expressed in John's Gospel: "But to all who received

---

43. *Commentary on John 1:12.* CNTC 4:18.

him, who believed in his name, he gave power to become children of God" (John 1:12).

Calvin wrote that "we believe in Christ when He is preached to us." This is the "usual way by which the Lord leads us to faith." Today, in the common experience of preaching the gospel of Jesus Christ, in churches and in many other contexts, faith is born and nourished by the power of the Holy Spirit. To put it simply, as Calvin said, "Christ offers Himself to us through the Gospel and we receive Him by faith."

The gospel, as we know it through the Scriptures and as it is proclaimed through preaching, is the message of who Jesus Christ *is* and what Jesus Christ *did*. The four Gospels tell the story of Jesus—his teachings, his miracles, his interactions with his contemporaries. The message of Jesus Christ—called the "gospel" because it is "good news"—is the declaration of the meaning of these events and the meaning of Jesus Christ himself. As we read of Jesus and hear the gospel proclaimed, we respond to the good news of Jesus by believing in him as our Savior from sin and commit ourselves to him as the Lord of our lives. We receive Christ by faith!

JOHN 3:1–16

44

The Heart of God Poured Out in Love

> The true looking of faith, I say, is placing Christ before one's eyes and beholding in Him the heart of God poured out in love.[44]

++++

Imagine what it would have been like to have been a resident of Jerusalem on the day Jesus of Nazareth was crucified. Crucifixions, carried out by the occupying Roman government, were common at that time. They were a cruel, humiliating, and excruciatingly painful way of death. Crucifixions were public displays of governmental power and were hoped to be a deterrent to all who would break laws and challenge Roman power.

On that Friday, when Jesus was crucified between two criminals (Luke 23:32–33), his suffering would have looked like that of others who were crucified on the hill outside the city.

---

44. *Commentary on John 3:16.* CNTC 4:74.

But more was going on here than met the eye. The conviction of Christ's followers—who became the church of Jesus Christ—is that on that cross where Christ died, Jesus was securing salvation, the forgiveness of sins and eternal life for the world. The most famous verse in the Bible says, "For God so loved the world that he gave his only Son, so that everyone who believes in him may not perish but may have eternal life" (John 3:16). In his crucifixion, believers receive eternal life.

Calvin wrote that "the true looking of faith, I say, is placing Christ before one's eyes and beholding in Him the heart of God poured out in love." In the cross of Jesus, the heart of God is poured out in love for the world.

This is why the death of Jesus is so important and why the cross is the central symbol of Christianity. When we look at the cross of Jesus, we see more than just another death in an endless series of Roman executions. We see, in the cross of Jesus, the depth of God's love poured out . . . for us!

JOHN 3:17–21

45

Faith Is the Root of Good Works

For we know that faith is the root from which good works spring.[45]

++++

One of the important issues during the sixteenth-century Protestant Reformation was the relationship between faith and works. The emphasis of Martin Luther and what became the viewpoint of Protestants is that salvation or justification comes through one's faith in Jesus Christ. This brings the forgiveness of sins: "Those who believe in him are not condemned" (John 3:18) says the Gospel of John. A relationship of love and trust with God, through Jesus Christ, given by the power of the Holy Spirit, enables believers—now "children of God" (John 1:12)—to do "good works" (Eph 2:10). Good works are an *expression* of faith, not the *cause* of faith. Calvin put this clearly and succinctly. He wrote that "the general

---

45. *Commentary on John* 3:21. CNTC 4:77.

teaching of Scripture" is that "faith is the root from which good works spring."

Our impetus is to express our faith by serving God as vigorously as possible. We devote our time and energies to doing what God wants us to do. This takes shape through our vocation, our "calling by God," to carry out God's will in this world. Our "good works" are oriented toward the needs of others. We seek to live the commandment to "love your neighbor" (Lev 19:18; Matt 19:19) and to serve others, as Jesus said—and did (Matt 20:28).

We do not consciously seek to do "good works." If we did, we would be implicitly assuming that good works may "save us" or gain us "status" before God. Our good works follow from our faith as a natural expression of our love for Christ—not as a way to show our "goodness" or earn God's favor. In Jesus' parable of the last judgment (Matt 25:31–46), those who are "righteous" are surprised when their "good works" are recognized (Matt 25:37–39). We should be surprised as well!

When I was hungry, you fed me.

JOHN 3:31–36

46

God Takes the Initiative

It is the property of faith to rest upon God and to be established in His Word. For there can be no assent unless God takes the initiative.[46]

++++

An emphasis of John Calvin, and after him the Reformed theological tradition, is that in salvation it is God who takes the initiative. We see this in John 3:16: "For God so loved the world that he gave his only Son, so that everyone who believes in him may not perish but may have eternal life." It is God who, in overflowing love for the world, sent Jesus Christ—the "only Son"—so that through faith in him, the world can be saved.

Humans cannot save themselves—establish a relationship of love and trust with God—by their own efforts, by themselves. If salvation from the power of human sin is ever to be achieved, God

---

46. *Commentary on John* 3:33. CNTC 4:83.

must make the first move. God must take the initiative to provide a savior. This is Jesus Christ.

We receive the gift of salvation through faith. Through faith we accept God's love and forgiveness of our sin. Faith is focused on God and God's promises, not on human abilities. We receive Christ by faith, and this too is the work of God. As Calvin wrote, "It is the property of faith to rest upon God and to be established in His Word. For there can be no assent unless God takes the initiative."

Faith is the gift of God, as Paul wrote: "For by grace you have been saved through faith, and this is not your own doing; it is the gift of God—not the result of works, so that no one may boast" (Eph 2:8–9). The Holy Spirit initiates faith—what God does for us. All praise and thanksgiving for salvation goes to God. God takes the initiative, doing for us what we could never do for ourselves. Praise God!

JOHN 5:2-9

47

Following the Word with Eyes Shut

> We only show our teachableness when we follow the bare Word with our eyes shut, though it does not seem worth our while.... God acts contrary to human reason in such a way that He never disappoints or plays with us.[47]

++++

Our Christian faith is an incredible journey with our lives focused on following Jesus Christ. We learn as we go, seeking to be "teachable," as Calvin often wrote. We want to do God's will and follow God's desires for us in Christ, by the power of the Holy Spirit.

God's word in Scripture helps us know God's will for us. We follow Scripture, the "bare Word," with our "eyes shut," says Calvin. He is urging us to trust God's word and be willing to follow where we are led, even when we don't know where that will be or how God will guide us. Sometimes this "does not seem worth our while" since we cannot perceive what God is doing in our lives

---

47. *Commentary on John 5:4.* CNTC 4:119.

God is a contrarian —   Man plans,
God laughs.

or how God is leading us. God may move us in ways contrary to our reason or in ways that are apparently futile. But God does not disappoint us!

Jesus healed a man who had been ill for thirty-eight years. While the man sought help to get to healing waters, Jesus instead asked him if he wanted to be healed. He did; and he was healed by Jesus' word (John 5:8). He trusted Jesus' word and was "made well" and "began to walk" (5:9). Jesus' power enabled his healing even when his reason and no experience in his life made it seem as though this would happen.

The man followed Jesus' word "with eyes shut." God may act for us contrary to our reason or our expectations. With a teachable spirit, we follow God's word and are "made well!"

Lord, Let us open our hearts and minds to your call. While it might be uncomfortable and contrary to what we think, keep us open to what you would have us do.

In his name,
Amen

JOHN 5:10–16

48

Stirred to Gratitude

> We wickedly abuse God's gifts unless we are stirred to gratitude.[48]

++++

After Jesus healed the man who had been ill for thirty-eight years and by his word enabled the man to be "made well" and "walk" (John 5:11), he found the man in the temple. Jesus said to him, "See, you have been made well! Do not sin any more, so that nothing worse happens to you" (5:14).

Calvin saw that in this comment that Jesus is conveying "a very useful lesson." Jesus meant, said Calvin, that "we wickedly abuse God's gifts unless we are stirred to gratitude." Gratitude is our response to what God has done for us in Christ. Jesus was reminding the man that "he had been healed to remember the grace he had received and worship God his Saviour all his life." We remember grace given to us, in gratitude.

48. *Commentary on John 5:14*. CNTC 4:121.

Indeed, said Calvin, "the general purpose both of our redemption and all God's gifts is to keep us entirely devoted to him." Our whole lives, as those who have received redemption and all God's grace in Jesus Christ, are to be devoted solely to God in Christ. All our service as disciples of Jesus arises from our deepest gratitude for what Christ has done for us. We are stirred to gratitude as we use God's gifts to us gratefully. Without gratitude we "wickedly abuse God's gifts." We treat them as normal parts of life or as what we deserve, rather than seeing them as the wondrous love of God given to us in God's grace.

Worship helps us express our gratitude for grace received. Worship focuses our attention on God and what God has done. Our prayers, praise, and response to God's word are expressions of grateful devotion—a devotion that leads us to follow Jesus with wholehearted commitment and devotion as grateful disciples!

John 6:1-14

49

Blessed When We Serve

God blesses our labour when we serve one another.[49]

++++

The miracle of Jesus feeding the 5,000 is found in all four Gospels. It is a dramatic depiction of the power of God to do that which is beyond our thought and to provide food for people in need.

Before the disciples distributed the five loaves and two fish, Jesus prayed over them: "Then Jesus took the loaves, and when he had given thanks, he distributed them to those who were seated; so also the fish, as much as they wanted" (John 6:11).

From this we learn we should always give thanks—especially for our food (see 1 Tim 4:4). It is God's gift. Jesus had given thanks for the meager food and it became food sufficient to feed all the people. Calvin wrote: "By Christ's wanting the bread given to the disciples to increase in their hands, we are taught that God blesses

---

49. *Commentary on John 6:11.* CNTC 4:147.

our labour when we serve one another." This is a word for us, always. God blesses our labors when we serve one another!

Sometimes we hear people say, "That was a thankless task." They did not receive thanks or recognition for what they did. But we can be sure that when we serve others, our labors will be blessed by God, even if they are not acknowledged by others or those we serve. This is a great impetus to serve others as disciples of Jesus. We serve others without concern about whether they acknowledge us or not. God knows our service. God blesses our service and labors. This is what we need, all we need!

This frees us to serve God fully, without hope for reward or even acknowledgment by others. We serve God in Jesus Christ, and our work for Christ is blessed by God. We never know how God will use our service for others. But we trust God will bless what we do, and this is our joy!

JOHN 6:22-34

50

Only Believe

Faith alone is enough, for God requires of us only that we believe.[50]

++++

There is a religious or theological question that is basic for all of us. It is the question asked by members of a crowd that saw Jesus perform the miracle of feeding 5,000 people (John 6:1–14). When some of them tracked Jesus down, they asked him, very simply: "What must we do to perform the works of God" (6:28)?

We wonder: What must we do to be doing the "works of God?" What does God require? What are the actions God finds acceptable? How can we do these "works of God?"

But Jesus' response brings a different focus. Instead of listing a lot of "things to do" to be doing the "works" of God, Jesus calls the people back to what is singular and is most basic. Jesus answered them, "This is the work of God, that you believe in him

50. *Commentary on John* 6:29. CNTC 4:155.

whom he has sent" (6:29). As Calvin commented: "They had spoken of works; Christ brings them back to one work, that is, faith. By this He means that whatever men undertake without faith is useless and vain, but that faith alone is enough, for God requires of us only that we believe." Only believe! This is the one action that saves us. Only believe in the one whom God has sent: Jesus Christ!

"Faith alone" was a motto of Martin Luther's during the Protestant Reformation. We are not saved and nor do we gain salvation by doing thing after thing, piling up "good works" to try to "get right" with God. Instead of "many works," there is only one "work" that counts: faith in Jesus Christ.

Calvin went on to say that even if people "wear themselves out all their lives, they are only playing at work unless faith in Christ is the rule of their lives." Only believe!

JOHN 10:11-18

51

Wolves Within and Sheep Without

Augustine's observation on this passage is indeed true. Even as there are many wolves within the church, so there are many sheep without.[51]

++++

This passage begins with the beloved saying of Jesus: "I am the good shepherd" (John 10:11). When we hear these words, we think of Christ as our shepherd, of Christ as the good shepherd of all those who hear his voice (see John 10:27).

Jesus went on to say that as the good shepherd (10:14) he lays down his life for his sheep (10:15). Then he said, "I have other sheep that do not belong to this fold. I must bring them also and they will listen to my voice" (10:16).

Calvin believed Jesus was referring to gentiles here: "Christ's office as a Shepherd is not restricted to the confines of Judaea, but is far wider." Then he went on to refer to the truth of an observation

51. *Commentary on John 10:16.* CNTC 4:266.

of Augustine: "Even as there are many wolves within the church, so there are many sheep without."

For Calvin, referring to "the secret election of God," we are "already God's sheep before we are aware that He is our Shepherd." This is true for all who are Christians in the sheepfold.

When we look around today, we see there are "wolves" within the church—those who do not live out their profession of Christian faith. But there are also "many sheep without." There are those elected by God who, at this point, are not joined into the body of Christ, the people of God. Not yet; but maybe soon . . .

A word for us, too: Are we sure we are "in" the sheepfold? Also: Are we sure others are "not in" the sheepfold?

It is not up to us to determine who is "in" and who is "out" of the sheepfold. We hear and respond to the voice of the good shepherd, who loves us and lay down his life for his sheep.

JOHN 14:15–17

52

The Holy Spirit Is Known by Faith

> But Christ's words show that nothing relating to the Holy Spirit can be learned by human reason, but that He is known only by the experience of faith.[52]

++++

We often neglect to think about the Holy Spirit. The Spirit may be "the forgotten member" of the Trinity!

The Spirit's work is wider and deeper than we can know. The Spirit brings us to faith, sustains us in faith, and leads us in ministries of witness and service in the world. The Spirit's activities are God's ongoing presence in the world. By the Spirit, we are united by faith to Jesus Christ and enjoy a spiritual union with him. Through the Spirit's actions, the providence of God is carried out and we are led into God's ways to carry out God's purposes. So the Spirit is indispensable! The Spirit goes before us, surrounds us, and

---

52. *Commentary on John 14:17.* CNTC 5:83.

is within us to enable us to live as the children of God. To Paul, "all who are led by the Spirit of God are children of God" (Rom 8:14).

The work of the Spirit is not apparent to those without faith. Jesus said, "This is the Spirit of truth, whom the world cannot receive, because it neither sees him nor knows him. You know him, because he abides with you, and he will be in you" (John 14:17). We know the Spirit's work by faith. Calvin said, "Christ's words show that nothing relating to the Holy Spirit can be learned by human reason, but that He is known only by the experience of faith." Outside the experience of faith, things appear to happen "at random"; love occurs as just "something that happens" in life; or care is offered to you, without any understanding of why this should be so.

But the Holy Spirit is known by faith; and that makes all the difference! We see and experience the Spirit at work around us, among us, and within us. By faith, the world is always alive! God's Spirit is everywhere!

JOHN 17:1-5

53

The Face of Jesus Christ

God is known only in the face of Jesus Christ, who is His living and express image.[53]

++++

Where do we see God?

The Christian answer is that we see God *in Jesus Christ*, whom God has sent into the world to save sinners. As Jesus told his disciples: "And this is eternal life, that they may know you, the only true God, and Jesus Christ whom you have sent" (John 17:3). Calvin wrote that "God is known only in the face of Jesus Christ, who is His living and express image."

When we want to know what God is like, we look at the face of Jesus Christ—what he said, what he did. Jesus is "the human face of God." This is the incarnation: God has become a human being in the person of Jesus Christ, the eternal word of God (John 1:1-14).

---

53. *Commentary on John 17:3.* CNTC 5:136.

Calvin said Jesus is God's "living and express image." Genesis 1:27 says God created humanity to be in the "image" of God. One way of understanding this is to say God created humans "to image" God. We are to live as God wants us to live. We are to reflect God's glory and serve God—with our whole lives.

The human being who has reflected God's glory and served God perfectly throughout his life is Jesus Christ. Jesus shows us what a life lived in perfect obedience to the will of God looks like. When tempted, as we are, Jesus remained faithful to God's purposes (Heb 4:15). When faced with suffering and impending death for the sake of being faithful to God, Jesus prayed, "not my will but yours be done" (Luke 22:42).

When we look into the face of Jesus Christ, we see God. So we follow Jesus' will and ways for our lives. Jesus reveals God to us by reaching out to us: he has become one of us—a person. Look to Jesus!

JOHN 17:6–19

54

Predestination Is Shown in Christ Alone

Faith flows from the eternal predestination of God, and that therefore it is not given to all indiscriminately, since not all belong to Christ.... For in itself the predestination of God is hidden; and it is manifested to us in Christ alone.[54]

++++

John Calvin is associated with the doctrine of predestination or election. Calvin emphasized that God eternally elects those who are saved and incorporated into Jesus Christ by faith. He believed the Bible teaches not all persons are saved. Not all people have faith in Jesus Christ as their Lord and Savior. Those who do believe and have faith do so because of God's election and grace. When salvation is received, it comes by God's election or predestination, and is not of human merit or deserving. Salvation is by *God's* work—by

54. *Commentary on John 17:6.* CNTC 5:139.

the Holy Spirit—in bringing faith in Christ. Election or predestination is another way of saying that salvation is by God's grace.

The focus of predestination is always Jesus Christ. Calvin called Christ the "mirror" of election.[55] This means if we want to know if we are elected by God, we ask: "Do I believe in Jesus Christ?" Faith in Christ is the expression of election. Those who believe are elected by God and receive the gift of eternal life through faith.

Calvin expressed these emphases as he interpreted Jesus' prayer for his disciples: "Faith flows from the eternal predestination of God, and that therefore it is not given to all indiscriminately, since not all belong to Christ. . . . For in itself the predestination of God is hidden; and it is manifested to us in Christ alone." It is to Christ, said Calvin, that we must "turn our eyes if we are to be certain that we are of the number of God's children." As Jesus said, "I have made your name known to those whom you gave me" (John 17:6). Predestination is shown in Christ alone!

---

55. *Institutes* 3.24.5.

JOHN 20:19-23

55

What Is Most Important

Nothing is more important for us than to be able to believe definitely that our sins do not come into remembrance before God.[56]

++++

We all like to receive good news. We got the new job. Our child is getting married. The doctor says my test results were fine. These are slices of life that make us glad, that bring relief, that give us hope.

The best "good news" we can receive is to know our sin is forgiven by God. Sin is a daily part of our lives. We break God's laws, go our own ways, fall short of being the people God wants us to be. So we know sin; and our guilt can be strong.

To be able to believe our sins are forgiven by God marks one of the most important aspects of our lives: how we stand in relation to our creator and the God who loves us. To sin against God's will

---

56. *Commentary on John 20:23.* CNTC 5:207.

for us is serious and brings us anguish. So the best news we can receive is what Calvin described when he wrote that "nothing is more important for us than to be able to believe definitely that our sins do not come into remembrance before God." Sins forgiven!

When God forgives sins, God no longer brings our sins to mind. As the psalmist prayed, "according to your abundant mercy blot out my transgressions" (Ps 51:1). Our sin is forgiven . . . and forgotten by God! This forgiveness expresses God's "abundant mercy." After his resurrection, Jesus appeared to his disciples and sent them on their mission. Their message was that sin can be forgiven, as the disciples themselves could declare in the name of Jesus (John 20:23).

"Nothing is more important for us" than to believe our sins are forgiven. Are we forgiven by God? Do we know this good news? This is the most important good news of our lives!

ACTS 23:12-35

56

No Way . . . Yes, Way!

Therefore although no ordinary way of obtaining deliverance is apparent to us, let us learn to lean on the Lord, who will find a way through impassable places.[57]

++++

An important work of God happened to Paul when he was imprisoned in Jerusalem (Acts 23:12–35). Religious leaders plotted to ambush Paul as he was to be taken before the council the next day. But "the son of Paul's sister" heard about the ambush. He told Paul who asked that his nephew be taken to the tribune. The nephew informed the tribune of the conspiracy plot to ambush Paul. The tribune arranged for Paul to be transported under armed guards to Felix the Governor that night. So the ambush plot was thwarted.

Calvin saw this story as showing that "God counters the plan of the ungodly as though by a flanking attack." The story is also "a mirror for our consideration." It shows God's providence protects

---

57. *Commentary on Acts 23:16*. CNTC 7:239.

us "because the promise remains unshakable, 'Not a hair of your head will be lost' etc. (Luke 21:18)." God helps and protects us.

Also, God acts in unexpected ways and by unexpected means, which strengthens our faith. For "who would have thought that the ambush was to be discovered by a lad, when the conspirators thought that they were the only ones who knew about it? Therefore although no ordinary way of obtaining deliverance is apparent to us, let us learn to lean on the Lord, who will find a way through impassable places."

God is the "Lord of impassable places!" When there appears to be no solution, no help, no way, God provides a way! For "nothing will be impossible with God" (Luke 1:37). What a story to bolster our faith. God can bring us safely through even circumstances that seem hopeless, where there is nothing we can do to help ourselves. But don't lose hope and faith. God helps and saves. God provides a path to deliverance: From "no way" to "yes, way!"

ACTS 28:23-30

57

The Kingdom of God

> The Kingdom of God is founded on, and consists in, the knowledge of the redemption procured by Christ.[58]

++++

When we hear the term "kingdom of God," we may wonder what is meant. It can seem rather vague. Sometimes it is said that when preachers need a sermon title for next week's worship service, they say: "The Kingdom of God." They are confident they can bring in almost any thought under that title!

The last verses of Acts describe Paul preaching in Rome, where he was "proclaiming the kingdom of God and teaching about the Lord Jesus Christ, with all boldness and without hindrance" (Acts 28:31). "The kingdom of God" is connected with "the Lord Jesus Christ," linking Christ with the kingdom. Calvin wrote that "the Kingdom of God is founded on, and consists in, the knowledge of the redemption procured by Christ."

---

58. *Commentary on Acts 28:31.* CNTC 7:314.

Early church theologians spoke of the "kingdom of God" as being Jesus Christ himself. It is a "self-kingdom" (Greek *autobasileia*). This meant Jesus, in who he was and what he did, constitutes the kingdom of God in himself, in the present. Calvin highlights this by focusing on the "redemption procured by Christ."

So, as we receive Christ's redemptive work by faith, we participate in the kingdom of God. This kingdom is at work in this world, here and now, as Christ is at work—even through us! The kingdom will be brought to consummation in the future, with the coming of Christ. As we pray: "Your kingdom come" (Matt 6:10).

Calvin saw our participation in the kingdom of God, now, as the beginning of "the heavenly life on earth," even as we "always desire to reach heaven." Day by day, as we minister in the name of Jesus, we live in the kingdom of God, which is already present in Christ, but still to come fully in God's future!

Romans 1:1–7

58

Jesus Christ: Divinity and Humanity

> The whole Gospel is contained in Christ.... Divinity and humanity are the two requisites which we must look for in Christ if we are to find salvation in Him.[59]

++++

Christianity is focused on Jesus Christ. We are called "Christians" because we are disciples of Jesus Christ. As Calvin wrote, Jesus Christ is "the One who is both the object and center of our whole faith." Indeed, "the whole Gospel is contained in Christ."

But who is Jesus Christ? There are many ways to answer that question. What the early church regarded as essential was to affirm that Jesus Christ was one person who had two natures. He was, at the same time, both divine and human. This made Jesus unique among all other persons who ever lived. Both these dimensions are necessary if Christ were to die for our sins and bring salvation. As Calvin put it, "Divinity and humanity are the two requisites which

---

59. *Commentary on Romans 1:3.* CNTC 8:15.

we must look for in Christ if we are to find salvation in Him. His divinity contains power, righteousness, and life, which are communicated to us by His humanity."

If Jesus were not divine, his death would have no power to save us and bring salvation. If Jesus were not human, he could not identify with us and share in the fullness of our humanity. Jesus was the promised Messiah, the "Son of God" (Rom 1:3–4). The message of who Jesus is and what Jesus has done is the "gospel concerning [God's] Son," the "good news" God promised and which is fulfilled in Jesus Christ.

Jesus is "Immanuel" (Matt 1:23): "God with us." In Christ, "the Word became flesh and lived among us" (John 1:14). Jesus knows us fully and intimately. He has the power to save us by his death and resurrection. This is the gospel!

ROMANS 6:1–4

59

New Creatures by Baptism

Baptism means that being dead to ourselves, we may become new creatures.[60]

++++

Paul asked the Roman Christians: "Do you not know that all of us who have been baptized into Christ Jesus were baptized into his death?" (Rom 6:3). By faith we are united to Jesus Christ and our existence now is a new existence because our whole lives have been dramatically changed! We have been baptized!

Being "baptized" into Christ's death means that we have rejected the claims of ourselves on our lives and have given our lives to the will and purposes of Jesus Christ. In short, said Calvin, "Baptism means that being dead to ourselves, we may become new creatures." We move from death to new life. Our "old selves" are destroyed; our "new selves" now emerge. As the waters of baptism are sprinkled over us, or as we are submerged underwater, we arise

60. *Commentary on Romans 6:4*. CNTC 8:122.

and receive new life—the life of Jesus Christ living in us by the power of the Holy Spirit. As Paul put it, "We have been buried with him by baptism into death, so that, just as Christ was raised from the dead by the glory of the Father, so we too might walk in newness of life." We are new creatures by baptism!

Whether our baptism is as infants or adults, we are new creatures by baptism. Baptism is the doorway of the life of faith, a life marked by discipleship and obedience to Jesus Christ. The sacrament of baptism is a sign of this new life. Baptism is a seal of the new life as we live by the power of God's Holy Spirit who unites us by faith throughout our lives of discipleship with Jesus Christ.

Baptism occurs for us once; but it has ongoing effects throughout our lives in all our days. We die to ourselves—daily—to become "new creatures" in Christ Jesus our Lord!

Romans 12:1-2

60

Knowledge of God's Will Is True Wisdom

The knowledge of God's will is true wisdom.[61]

++++

As we usually talk about it, there is a difference between "knowledge" and "wisdom." We think of knowledge as what we know—ideas, information about the world around us, various facts—whereas wisdom is knowledge filtered through experience—the ways in which knowledge is applied.

But there is a knowledge that goes beyond "facts," and a wisdom that is more than just our application of knowledge to our lives.

Calvin speaks fully about the "knowledge of God." This is the most important knowledge we can have. It is to know God as a reality; and beyond that to know who God is—what God is like

---

61. *Commentary on Romans 12:2.* CNTC 8:265.

and what God has done. To know the true and living God is the deepest and most important knowledge we can have.

"True wisdom" is this knowledge of God as it bears on our lives—our decisions, our values, our ways of living. This wisdom comes from God and is imparted to us in the Scriptures and supremely in Jesus Christ.

When interpreting Paul's words to the Romans—"Be transformed by the renewing of your minds, so that you may discern what is the will of God" (Rom 12:2)—Calvin wrote, "The knowledge of God's will is true wisdom." Knowing God and how God wants us to live is the wisdom that gives life its meaning and significance.

Our minds, as sinners, are opposed to God and we do not care about God's will. By the renewal of our minds by Jesus Christ, through faith, we receive a knowledge of God and knowing God's will becomes our true wisdom.

What knowledge could be more important to us than knowing who God is and what God's will for our lives is? This is our true wisdom—that which we need to know and experience more than anything else. Know God's will and be truly wise!

ROMANS 13:8-10

61

God's Law Is to Encourage Love

By all His commandments God had no other purpose than to instruct us in the duty of love, we ought to strive to attain it in every way.... The object of the whole law is to encourage us to cultivate love for one another.[62]

++++

When we think of the commandments of God, we may shudder! We think of thunderbolts from Mt. Sinai and those Ten Commandments which we are never able to obey. The commandments of God condemn us to lives of guilt. We break the commandments and forever fall short of living as God commands.

But overall, there is a greater purpose to God's law and commandments. The law does condemn us, but Jesus Christ has come to give God's grace and to save us through faith, and not by obedience to God's law. As Paul wrote, "the law of the Spirit of life in

---

62. *Commentary on Romans 13:9.* CNTC 8:285.

Christ Jesus has set you free from the law of sin and of death" (Rom 8:2).

The purpose of the law is "summed up in the word, 'Love your neighbor as yourself'" (Rom 13:9). For "the one who loves another has fulfilled the law" (13:8). God's law is to encourage us to love one another. We do not do them harm; instead we actively love them. Calvin put it this way: "By all His commandments God had no other purpose than to instruct us in the duty of love, we ought to strive to attain it in every way.... The object of the whole law is to encourage us to cultivate love for one another."

Think of God's law this way! God's commandments are aimed at encouraging us to show us how God wants us to live: to live by the law of love! This is what we see in Jesus Christ himself—the one who loved God and others, fully. We love others as an expression of our love for God in Christ. We strive to attain love in every way!

1 CORINTHIANS 3:10–15

62

Church Is Founded on Christ Alone

> The Church must quite definitely be founded on Christ alone.... The fundamental doctrine, which it is forbidden to overthrow, is that we might learn Christ. For Christ is the one and only foundation of the Church.[63]

++++

Of all the groups and institutions with which we are affiliated, the church is different and unique.

The distinctiveness of the church is that it is the only institution which looks to Jesus Christ as its foundation. As Paul wrote to the Corinthians: "For no one can lay any foundation other than the one that has been laid; that foundation is Jesus Christ" (1 Cor 3:11). As we sing in "The Church's One Foundation," a hymn which is based on this verse, "The church's one foundation is Jesus Christ her Lord."

---

63. *Commentary on 1 Corinthians 3:11*. CNTC 9:74.

The implications of the church being grounded in Jesus Christ and looking to him as its Lord are many. Most basically, the church gets its character and mission from its Lord. What the church is and does must be consistent with the life and teachings of Jesus. The church is to "learn Christ." As Calvin put it, "The Church must quite definitely be founded on Christ alone. . . . The fundamental doctrine, which it is forbidden to overthrow, is that we might learn Christ. For Christ is the one and only foundation of the Church."

Despite all temptations to accommodate itself to contemporary culture or political perspectives, the church is to look to Christ. We are to hear his continuing word, by the Holy Spirit, for serving Jesus Christ in mission and ministry. We are to "live Christ." The church understands itself as serving Christ in this world and following God's will as the people of God. This is who we are and what we are called to do. Rejoice that our lives in the church are built on the sure foundation of Jesus Christ our Lord!

1 CORINTHIANS 11:23-26

63

At the Table: God's Boundless Love

As often as we approach the Holy Table, we may lift up our hearts in acknowledgement of the boundless love of God towards us, and be inflamed with true gratitude to Him.[64]

++++

Part of the liturgy for celebrating the Lord's Supper is often "The Great Prayer of Thanksgiving." Here the prayer rehearses the great actions of God in history and redemption, as we remember with thanksgiving all God has done. Jesus' own action at the Last Supper was that after he "took a loaf of bread," he gave thanks (1 Cor 11:23-24). We give thanks as Jesus did.

Calvin wrote that at the Last Supper, "Christ is giving thanks to His Father for His mercy towards the human race, and His priceless gift of redemption." Jesus' prayer was for us humans and for the gift of redemption to be received in Christ's death on the

---

64. *Commentary on 1 Corinthians 11:24.* CNTC 9:243.

cross. We receive, with deepest thanks, that which God has done in providing salvation for us.

Then, said Calvin, Jesus "encourages us, by His example, so that as often as we approach the Holy Table, we may lift up our hearts in acknowledgement of the boundless love of God towards us, and be inflamed with true gratitude to Him."

When we see the Lord's table spread before us in the church, the words of the gospel should ring in our ears! When we receive the bread and wine in communion—the body and blood of Jesus Christ—our hearts are gladdened as we praise and thank God for the "boundless love" shown in Jesus Christ. This is the greatest love we can ever experience. The Supper is a means by which that love becomes real and effective for us.

Our response is gratitude—deepest and true gratitude! Our hearts are "inflamed" in thanks for that unlimited love God has given each of us. Receive and celebrate God's boundless love in Jesus Christ!

1 Corinthians 12:27–31

64

No Useless Church Members

Even the least significant of believers does in fact bear fruit relative to his slender resources, so that there is no such person as a useless member of the Church.[65]

++++

Oftentimes we feel like rather insignificant Christians. We are part of the church and do what we can in serving Christ. But it may seem we are not really making a difference or having an impact. It's easy to sink into feeling that others have received many more gifts and talents to use, so what we do feels insignificant by comparison.

But take heart! Paul tells us that in the church we are all part of "the body of Christ and individually members of it" (1 Cor 12:27). No matter who we are or what our gifts may be, we are members of the body of Christ and we serve Christ by who we are and what we do.

65. *Commentary on 1 Corinthians 12:27.* CNTC 9:269.

Calvin captured this when he wrote that "even the least significant of believers does in fact bear fruit relative to his slender resources, so that there is no such person as a useless member of the Church." There are no useless church members!

We use the gifts we've been given and use our talents and resources however we can in carrying out the mission and ministry of Jesus Christ through the church. We are not called on to "do great things." We are called to be faithful in employing our gifts for the sake of Christ and working for "building up the body of Christ" (Eph 4:12). We are not all given the same gifts, and we should not be "jealous" of those who appear to have more gifts or different gifts than ours. We use what we have been given as "servants of Christ" (1 Cor 4:1). We trust God to use our gifts and our efforts for the sake of Christ. This is our calling!

1 CORINTHIANS 13

65

The Most Excellent Way

The most excellent way then is where love is the controlling power in all our actions. . . . All virtues count for nothing without love.[66]

++++

A biblical passage often read at weddings is 1 Corinthians 13, Paul's chapter on love. This is usually applied to the love a marrying couple have for each other. Its scope, however, is much broader. Love stands as what Paul called, at the end of 1 Corinthians 12, "a still more excellent way."

This most excellent way is the way of love. Paul spoke about the upbuilding of the church through the various gifts given to those in the church. But greater than all specific gifts for the church's benefit is this "more excellent way"—which is a way of Christian living for all members of the body of Christ. All can follow the way of love as the mark of Christian living. Paul begins

66. *Commentary on 1 Corinthians 13:1*. CNTC 9:274.

by saying that "if I speak in the tongues of mortals and of angels, but do not have love, I am a noisy gong or a clanging cymbal" (13:1). He ends by saying that among faith, hope, and love—which "abide"—"the greatest of these is love" (13:13).

Calvin wrote that "the most excellent way then is where love is the controlling power in all our actions. . . . All virtues count for nothing without love." Love is at the center of our personalities and our actions. It is greater than all else because it reflects the very nature of God (1 John 4:8,16). Love is the "fulfilling of the law" (Rom 13:10) and "from God's point of view," there is "nothing, no matter how wonderful or extraordinary it may be," that is "not ruined" by "the absence of love." Love is not an option for the Christian; it is an absolute necessity. Love is to control all our actions. This "most excellent way" is the standard by which "all our actions are to be judged." Let us love!

1 CORINTHIANS 15:12–20

66

The Foundation of the Gospel

Let us therefore remember that the main foundation of the whole Gospel is the death and resurrection of Christ.[67]

++++

Jesus Christ is remembered for many things. His miraculous birth is celebrated every year at Christmas. His teachings are among the most wise and penetrating things ever said. His miracles caused amazement in those who witnessed them. By all accounts, Jesus would take his place among the world's greatest persons.

But the church has gone beyond this in its belief, *far* beyond. All these dimensions of Jesus are important. But even more important are his death and resurrection. The church—beginning in the pages of the New Testament—has seen these two inseparably related events to be key, to be foundational to the person of Jesus Christ and to the gospel the church proclaims.

67. *Commentary on 1 Corinthians 15:14.* CNTC 9:319.

Calvin wrote: "Let us therefore remember that the main foundation of the whole Gospel is the death and resurrection of Christ." Christ's death brings salvation, the forgiveness of sins, and eternal life. Christ's resurrection is the preview of our resurrection and the establishment of God's eternal reign and the new world God is bringing forth. Christ's resurrection establishes the validity of Christ's death. Christ's death is the beginning of new life for those who believe in Christ and in whose lives the Holy Spirit seals faith. Christ's death and resurrection are inextricably bound up together!

Christian faith is grounded in these two acts of God in Christ. Paul wrote that "if Christ has not been raised, then our proclamation has been in vain and your faith has been in vain" (1 Cor 15:14). If Christ died and was not raised, there is no salvation. Christ's resurrection after his death vindicates his death and brings us into the glory of eternal life forever. The sure foundation of our faith is Christ's death and resurrection!

1 CORINTHIANS 15:21-22

67

To Restore Everything

For He came to restore everything which had been brought to ruin in Adam.[68]

++++

First Corinthians 15 has sometimes been called the "spinal column" of the New Testament. It boldly proclaims the resurrection of Jesus Christ as the beginning of the resurrection of the dead and the proof of our own coming resurrections. Paul declares: "But in fact Christ has been raised from the dead, the first fruits of those who have died" (1 Cor 15:20). And as Calvin wrote, "The power of Christ's resurrection is extended to all of us."

Then Paul draws a contrast between "Adam"—the first person—and Jesus Christ. Sin and death came to the whole human race by the sin of Adam. But now, "the resurrection of the dead has also come through a human being; for as all die in Adam, so all will be made alive in Christ" (15:21-22). The curse of Adam has

68. *Commentary on 1 Corinthians 15:21-22*. CNTC 9:323.

been removed by the resurrection of Christ. The effects of human sin have been set right by the resurrection of Jesus. Calvin wrote that Jesus "came to restore everything which had been brought to ruin in Adam."

This is a word to bring us joy and sustaining faith! Theologically, physical death is no longer "the last word" in human existence. Resurrection is coming! Eternal life is our ultimate destiny!

Even the world as we know it—"fallen creation," affected by the results of sin—will be transformed. Finally, there will be a "new heaven and a new earth" (Rev 21:1). At the "end," Christ "hands over the kingdom to God the Father, after he has destroyed every ruler and every authority and power" (1 Cor 15:25). In the end, God will "be all in all" (15:28).

What a magnificent vision! And what an everlasting hope and blessed promise for all our days . . . forever! Christ restores everything ruined in this life and opens God's eternal future!

2 CORINTHIANS 5:6–10

68

A Better Hope

But we live with a quiet mind and go on to meet death without hesitation because a better hope is laid up for us.[69]

++++

We often think that we are shaped by our past, and so we are, to some degree. Our genes, our parents, our experiences all have effects and influence how we view life.

But do we realize that we are also shaped by our view of the future? What we believe about what lies ahead has a shaping effect on us as well. If we see the future as bleak and foreboding; our attitudes and actions will be affected. If we don't believe the future holds any promise, then why bother to get out of bed in the morning?

Paul said Christians are "always confident; even though we know that while we are at home in the body we are away from the

---

69. *Commentary on 2 Corinthians 5:6.* CNTC 10:69.

Lord" (2 Cor 5:6). Now, as we live life here on earth—not in the direct presence of God in heaven—we can be "always confident." Why? Because we "walk by faith, not by sight" (5:7) and believe God has given the Holy Spirit as a "guarantee" that our mortal lives will be swallowed up into our lives lived eternally with God. After death, we will "be away from the body and at home with the Lord" (5:8). As Calvin commented, "We live with a quiet mind and go on to meet death without hesitation because a better hope is laid up for us."

A better hope! This is what we need. We need a hope that enables us to meet death "without hesitation." This death-defying attitude can come only from a "better hope" that looks beyond death to the eternal life promised to us in Jesus Christ (John 3:15, 16).

Our view of the future shapes us now, every day. Our "better hope" is God's promise of "eternal life through Jesus Christ our Lord" (Rom 5:21)!

2 CORINTHIANS 5:16–21

69

The Quarrel Is Resolved

> This is the main purpose of the Gospel, that, although we are by nature children of wrath, the quarrel between God and us can be resolved and we can be received by Him into His grace.[70]

++++

A central passage of the New Testament is Paul's great description of the reconciliation brought by Jesus Christ (2 Cor 5:16–21). This passage is so significant since it speaks about the deepest realities we know—God's relationship with the world and our relationship with God.

Key are Paul's words: "All this is from God, who reconciled us to himself through Christ, and has given us the ministry of reconciliation" (2 Cor 5:18). On this verse, Calvin wrote: "This is the main purpose of the Gospel, that, although we are by nature

---

70. *Commentary on 2 Corinthians 5:18.* CNTC 10:77.

children of wrath, the quarrel between God and us can be resolved and we can be received by Him into His grace."

Throughout the Bible, God and humanity stand in relationship. Since Genesis 3, this relationship has been defined by human sin—humanity going its own way; each human focused on the self instead of on doing God's will or serving other people. Paul says we are "by nature children of wrath" (Eph 2:3).

But God in Christ has reached out to the world in love, elected people to receive salvation, and "resolved" the "quarrel between God and us." Now we can receive God's grace. Now we can receive salvation. Said Calvin, "What blessing could be more desirable than this!" When the quarrel is resolved, we are received into God's grace and receive reconciliation—being friends again with God. This is the gospel message we receive and proclaim to others. We are reconciled with God and receive "the ministry of reconciliation" (5:18). Our life's calling is to bring the reconciling message to Christ to a world in need; and work for the reconciliation of others with each other and with God.

2 CORINTHIANS 5:16–21

70

God Draws Near to Us in Christ

Whereas God had been before far distant from us, He has drawn near to us in Christ, and so Christ has been made to us the true Immanuel and His advent is the drawing near of God to men.[71]

++++

The Christmas message is that God's promise to the prophets has been fulfilled and that God's Son is born: "'And they shall name him Emmanuel,' which means 'God is with us'" (Matt 1:23). The angels proclaimed: "to you is born this day in the city of David a Savior, who is the Messiah, the Lord" (Luke 2:11). In John's Gospel we are told "the Word became flesh and lived among us" (1:14). In Jesus Christ, God has become a human being. Christ the Lord is with us in the here and now. As Jesus said, "the Father is in me and I am in the Father" (John 10:38).

---

71. *Commentary on 2 Corinthians 5:19*. CNTC 10:78.

Jesus Christ is God's divine revelation. He is the eternal Son of God who came to earth to do for humanity what we could never do for ourselves. Christ establishes the forgiveness of sin and grants eternal life. The is the church's christological message.

As Paul said, "In Christ God was reconciling the world to himself" (2 Cor 5:19). Calvin spoke simply of this reality: "Whereas God had been before far distant from us, He has drawn near to us in Christ, and so Christ has been made to us the true Immanuel and His advent is the drawing near of God to men." In Christ, God has drawn near to humanity. Through his death on the cross, reconciliation between sinful humans and God has come. Now humans can live by faith in fellowship with our loving creator.

This is the church's message for the world: God is revealed! Praise God he has drawn near to us in Christ!

2 CORINTHIANS 8:8-15

71

We Give from Christ's Example

> By Christ's example we are incited to beneficence so that we should not spare ourselves when our brethren require our help.[72]

++++

Love is at the core of Christian faith. God loves us. We love others. What links these two arms of love is Jesus Christ. God so loved the world and sent Jesus Christ (John 3:16). Jesus himself embodied love for others in his teachings (John 13:34) and in his actions, his miracles being primary examples.

Jesus' love is seen in his person. In his "richness" as the eternal Son of God (John 1:1), he became "poor" for the sake of bringing salvation and embodying God's love in his own self. As Paul wrote, "For you know the generous act [or "the grace"] of our Lord Jesus Christ, that though he was rich, yet for your sakes he became poor, so that by his poverty you might become rich" (2 Cor 8:9;

---

72. *Commentary on 2 Corinthians 8:9.* CNTC 10:110.

cf. Phil 2:5–11). By Christ's "poverty" we become "rich" out of the overflowing abundance of divine love.

In this, Jesus has given us the most important example of how we should love others. Calvin wrote that "by Christ's example we are incited to beneficence so that we should not spare ourselves when our brethren require our help." We show kindness, benevolence, care, and most of all, love for others because we follow the example of Jesus himself. The love we receive from Christ propels us to meet the needs of others because our needs have been met so fully in Christ's love for us. Calvin continued that Jesus has "enriched us so that we should not find it hard to take from our abundance what we may expend on behalf of our brethren." If we have received the greatest richness of all—salvation—how can we not give of the abundance of what we have to help others? We give from Christ's example, so let us follow him!

GALATIANS 3:10–14

72

Relying on Christ Alone

The law justifies him who fulfils all its commands, whereas faith justifies those who are destitute of the merit of works and rely on Christ alone.[73]

++++

One of the main issues in Paul's letter to the Galatians is how salvation is received. Is it by doing "works of the law" or by "believing what you heard" (Gal 3:5) by faith?

Paul argued that "all who rely on the works of the law" are under a "curse; for it is written, 'Cursed is everyone who does not observe and obey all the things written in the book of the law'" (3:10). If you can't keep the whole law of God, and disobey even one part, you are guilty of breaking the whole law of God. No salvation here!

Instead, says Paul, "it is evident that no one is justified before God by the law; for 'The one who is righteous will live by faith'"

---

73. *Commentary on Galatians 3:11.* CNTC 11:54.

(3:11). Here Paul was quoting the prophet Habakkuk who proclaimed, "the righteous live by their faith" (Hab 2:4; cf. Rom 1:17). We are justified by faith, by believing what God has said and done for us.

Interpreting Paul, Calvin commented that "the law justifies him who fulfils all its commands, whereas faith justifies those who are destitute of the merit of works and rely on Christ alone." The mode and means of justification is by faith—faith that trusts solely and completely in Jesus Christ, who died to bring us salvation. We are justified by faith in Christ alone, not trusting at all in our own efforts or merits. Salvation is God's gracious gift. Calvin continued to say that "to be justified by our own merit and by the grace of another are irreconcilable; the one is overthrown by the other." Our status of being "right with God" (justified) is by God's grace—we receive what we totally do not deserve: the gift of salvation! We rely on Jesus Christ alone!

Galatians 5:22–26

73

Only Glory in God

The heathen philosophers do not condemn every desire for glory. But among Christians, whoever is greedy for glory is justly accused of empty and foolish ambition, because he departs from true glory. It is only lawful for us to glory in God. Outside God it is always vanity.[74]

++++

In Galatians 5, Paul contrasts the works of the flesh with the "fruit of the Spirit" in comparing the way of living for those who do not know Jesus Christ with the ways those united with Christ by faith live as they are guided by the Spirit (Gal 5:22–26). Then, Paul wrote: "Let us not become conceited, competing against one another, envying one another" (5:26).

Conceit ("vain glory" in the King James Version), competition, and envying are not marks of Christian living; they belong to those who seek self-glorification. Calvin saw Paul's exhortation as important for his own time, and we can say for our time as

74. *Commentary on Galatians 5:25.* CNTC 11:107.

well! Calvin wrote: "Of the many evils existing in our society and particularly in the Church, ambition is the mother." Our ambition for self-promotion, for "celebrity," or to amount to more than others—this desire for our honor is counter to God's will. This applies in "spiritual things" as well.

Calvin notes that the heathen philosophers "do not condemn every desire for glory." But among Christians—those who are "greedy for glory" are accused of "empty and foolish ambition" because they are "departing from true glory." For "it is only lawful for us to glory in God." Our focus is fully and always on glorying in God—in who God is and what God has done. This is the true glory to which we commit and devote our lives. We only glory in God! For "outside God it is always vanity." What matters is not us, no matter what we achieve or what honors are bestowed upon us. What matters is God's glory in all things. All we are points to God!

EPHESIANS 1:3-14

74

God's Eternal Election

God's eternal election is the foundation and first cause both of our calling and of all the benefits which we received from God.[75]

++++

Theologians have long debated how salvation is accomplished. Does salvation come from God's eternal election, as God's gracious gift? Or, do we have goodness in ourselves that enables us to achieve salvation on the basis of what we can do?

Calvin, in the tradition of St. Augustine in the early church, believed salvation came totally by God's work. God gives us the gift of faith to receive Jesus Christ as our Lord and Savior, by the work of God's Holy Spirit.

Behind our responses of faith in Christ and receiving of all Christ has done for us is God's calling, and behind that is God's choosing or electing of us to receive salvation through Christ.

75. *Commentary on Ephesians 1:4.* CNTC 11:124.

Calvin wrote: "God's eternal election is the foundation and first cause both of our calling and of all the benefits which we received from God." This means simply that God has chosen us to receive salvation—the forgiveness of sins and a new status as God's child—as God's gift. Election comes to us through Jesus Christ in his death and resurrection. As Paul wrote, God "chose us in Christ before the foundation of the world to be holy and blameless before him in love" (Eph 1:4).

This means we attribute our salvation solely to the work of God! All we are given in Christ is by God's gracious election. We do not claim any goodness or merit within ourselves. Our calling to serve God is grounded in God choosing us to be God's people. This is the solid foundation of Jesus Christ. Through all the zigs and zags, the ups and downs of life, God's election stands firm and God is with us in Christ. All the salvation benefits we receive are from God alone! All glory be to God!

EPHESIANS 1:3-14

75

Our Highest End

The glory of God is the highest end, to which our sanctification is subordinate.[76]

++++

Paul's great passage about the spiritual blessings of Christ describes God's eternal election and its purpose: God "chose us in Christ before the foundation of the world to be holy and blameless before him in love" (Eph 1:4). We are chosen to be "holy and blameless" by living in love. Our Christian life, described in these terms, is what is called "sanctification," which literally means our growth in holiness.

Our sanctification seems the most important aspect of our Christian lives. We want to grow into the people God wants us to be; and serve God with holy lives expressing love, always. Sanctification is vital. There is no true Christian faith if we are not growing in our faith.

76. *Commentary on Ephesians 1:4.* CNTC 11:125.

But Paul points to more. He goes on to say that those who have "set their hope on Christ" are to "live for the praise of his glory" (1:12). We have a future redemption as "God's own people" and we live "to the praise of his glory" (1:14).

So there is a purpose beyond our own Christian growth. The purpose is that we live wholly for the glory of God! This is our primary purpose as God's people. Calvin wrote that "the glory of God is the highest end, to which our sanctification is subordinate." We look beyond our own relationship with God—important as it is—to the "highest end" of our lives, which is to be people who live "to the praise of his glory" (the term is used twice: 1:12, 14).

Do we see our primary purpose—the main, energizing purpose of our lives—as being to proclaim God's great glory, God's goodness, God's everlasting love? This is a purpose that captures the fullness of why God created us, elected us, and saves us. "Do everything for the glory of God," said Paul (1 Cor 10:31). Let's live to our "highest end!"

EPHESIANS 3:14–19

76

Certainty of Faith

The certainty of faith is knowledge ([Latin] *scientia*), but it is acquired by the teaching of the Holy Spirit, not by the acuteness of our own intellect.[77]

++++

How do we know God? This ageless question is one each of us has to answer.

There are a number of options. We can try to learn of God through our intellect, our powers of reason. Traditionally, there have been "logical arguments" for the existence of God. Yet, even if God could be "proven" this way, we would not know what the nature of God would be.

Some have sought to learn of God through human experience. As we experience various emotions and feelings, we may believe we are experiencing God. But what kind of God is this, and does this God "last" through our varying emotions and feelings?

---

77. *Commentary on Ephesians 3:19.* CNTC 11:169.

But Paul wrote that "the love of Christ surpasses knowledge" (Eph 3:19). We know God by faith in Jesus Christ, and we know Christ by the work of the Holy Spirit. As Calvin put it, "The certainty of faith is knowledge ([Latin] *scientia*), but it is acquired by the teaching of the Holy Spirit, not by the acuteness of our own intellect."

Since our faith is grounded in the work of God's Spirit as the Spirit brings us to a knowledge of God in Jesus Christ, we have a "certainty of faith." Our faith is not dependent on the weakness of our own intellects; or the limits and weaknesses of human reasoning. Our faith is not captive to our feelings or emotions—whatever they may be at any specific day or time in our lives.

Our faith is established by God's work through the Holy Spirit to bring us to faith in believing Jesus Christ is God's Son, who is our Lord and Savior. Our faith is sustained by the Spirit's ongoing work in our lives as we know and learn of Jesus Christ and as we live as his disciples.

EPHESIANS 4:1–16

77

Be Whatever We Are for Others

So if we wish to be considered in Christ, let no man be anything for himself, but let us all be whatever we are for others. This is accomplished by love; and where love does not reign, there is no edification of the Church, but a mere scattering.[78]

++++

The church is—or should be—built up by love. As Paul wrote in his great passage on unity in the body of Christ (Eph 4:1–16), Jesus Christ is the head of the church (4:15). The church is to "grow up in every way into him." Christ "promotes the body's growth in building itself up in love" (4:16).

Whatever growth in faith we experience, as members of the body of Christ, is to be directed to the whole body of believers in love, to the glory of Christ. Calvin asked what use there would be in a physical body if a leg or arm "grew to an enormous size" or "for the mouth to be stretched wider?" It would result in the

78. *Commentary on Ephesians 4:16.* CNTC 11:185.

affliction of "a harmful tumour." So, Calvin said, "if we wish to be considered in Christ, let no man be anything for himself, but let us all be whatever we are for others. This is accomplished by love; and where love does not reign, there is no edification of the Church, but a mere scattering."

No one in the church should tout what God is doing in one's life if that work of God is not expressed in the body of Christ. It is the work of love to promote the whole church's growth in love and service to Christ. Where love does not reign in the church, the church cannot "grow up in every way" into Christ.

We are to be whatever we are for others. Whatever gifts and blessings we have been given are there so we can express love for others in the church and for Christ. We are to be nothing for ourselves. But we are also to be "whatever we are for others!"

Philippians 1:19–26

78

Happy in Life and Death

> Assuredly it is Christ alone who makes us happy both in death and in life. . . . Let Christ be with us, and He will bless our life as well as our death, so that both will be happy and desirable for us.[79]

++++

Paul's letter to the Philippians is "the epistle of joy." Paul expresses the joy of living united to Jesus Christ by faith. Paul prays with joy (Phil 1:4), shares joy in faith (1:25), and anticipates the final joy of standing with others in the presence of Christ (4:1).

Paul lived in two worlds. He lived as Christ's disciple in the world of the here and now, but he also anticipated the heavenly world of living eternally in the presence of Christ. This led Paul to write that "for to me, living is Christ and dying is gain" (1:21).

Calvin said that for Paul, "Christ is the subject of both clauses" here. This means Christ is "declared to be gain to him both in life

---

79. *Commentary on Philippians 1:21.* CNTC 11:238.

and in death." Paul recognized the joy of living in Christ now. He also knew he would "depart" this life and "be with Christ" (1:23). This will be joy as well. Both living and dying are "gain" here, and beyond!

So Paul can be happy in life and death. Calvin wrote that "assuredly it is Christ alone who makes us happy both in death and in life. . . . Let Christ be with us, and He will bless our life as well as our death, so that both will be happy and desirable for us."

Knowing this gives us wonderful freedom! We are free to give our lives fully and totally to serving Jesus Christ, every day, in every way, right now. We find true joy as disciples of Jesus. We are also free to anticipate the future, eternal happiness we will share with the saints in praise of Jesus Christ. Christ blesses our life and death—this is the truest happiness!

PHILIPPIANS 4:4-7

79

Our Chief Desire

Unquestionably, gratitude will have the effect upon us that the will of God will be the chief sum of our desires.[80]

++++

Paul urged the Philippians not to worry about anything but "in everything by prayer and supplication with thanksgiving let your requests be made known to God" (Phil 4:6). This is advice for us as well. In all things, we should pray to God, making our requests known to the Lord. Our prayers are accompanied by thanksgiving to God. As Calvin said, "Paul joins thanksgiving with prayers."

An implication of Paul's words here, as Calvin points out, is that "it is as though he had said, that those things which are necessary for us ought to be desired from the Lord in such a way that we nevertheless subject our affections to His will, and give thanks while asking. And, unquestionably, gratitude will have the effect upon us that the will of God will be the chief sum of our desires."

80. *Commentary on Philippians 4:6*. CNTC 11:290.

Our prayers—with their desires—are offered as part of the greater and larger purpose of submitting ourselves to God's will. This is focused for us when we thank God along with petitioning or praying for our desires. In thanksgiving, we are acknowledging what God has done and what God will do. We want our prayers and desires to be part of God's will for us. As we thank God and are grateful to God, we subject ourselves to God's will and seek God's way.

Our deepest desire is to do the will of God. This was Jesus' way, even as he faced a torturous death: "not my will but yours be done" (Luke 22:42). Our prayers, offered with gratitude, will reflect this passionate desire and commitment. Because we are grateful to God, we seek to serve God, and we seek to follow God's will. This is our chief desire!

1 TIMOTHY 6:11–16

80

Called by God

Nothing can fill us with courage more than the knowledge that we have been called by God.[81]

++++

Being a Christian means giving one's life to the God revealed in Jesus Christ. As disciples of Jesus, we will be at odds with the culture around us in various way. We do not fit into the world's mold. We are transformed by Christ and "pursue righteousness, godliness, faith, love, endurance, gentleness" as Timothy is told (1 Tim 6:12). This is "the good fight of the faith" for which we are to contend.

Like Timothy, we are also to "take hold of the eternal life to which you were called." We can contend for Christian faith by holding on to the eternal life given us in Jesus Christ and which we receive through being called by God.

"Being called by God." This makes all the difference! Our salvation and the gifts we receive are given by the God who calls us

---

81. *Commentary on 1 Timothy 6:12.* CNTC 10:277.

into eternal life. Calvin wrote that "nothing can fill us with courage more than the knowledge that we have been called by God." Courage to continue in the faith and pursue the things of faith comes when we realize God has called us—called *me!*—to receive the greatest gift: eternal life in Jesus Christ. Calvin declares it should be "the strongest encouragement to us to be told, 'God hath called thee to eternal life.'" What deeper blessing can there be than to know eternal life is God's gift to us!

This courage launches us into serving Jesus Christ in this world, in word and deed. Calvin sees this as encouraging us "that our labour, which is under God's direction, and in which He stretches out His hand to us, will not be in vain" (cf. 1 Cor 15:58). Our service to Christ is meaningful and gains its significance because it is grounded in God's call. This is our confident assurance for dynamic discipleship. We are called by God!

Titus 3:4–8

81

What Is the Gospel?

The Gospel is the solemn proclamation of the presence of the Son of God revealed in the flesh to renew a fallen world, to restore men from death to life.[82]

++++

At the beginning of Calvin's commentaries on the first three Gospels, he wrote the essay "The Theme of the Gospel of Jesus Christ According to Matthew, Mark and Luke." Here, Calvin discussed the purpose behind the writing of the Gospels and said where the writings lead us.

The gospel is "the glad news" of Jesus Christ. In Christ, we find the fulfillment of the promises of God. Christ is "the pledge of all benefits that ever God has promised" and "we find in Him their full and substantial revelation." Jesus Christ reveals God.

In his death—the atonement—"sins are cleared" so "the curse and judgment of death should no longer weigh upon us." Then,

---

82. "The Theme of the Gospel of Jesus Christ according to Matthew, Mark and Luke." CNTC 1:xi.

"righteousness, salvation and entire felicity are based upon His rising again." Christ's death and resurrection bring salvation and eternal life (Titus 3:4–8).

Calvin wrote: "The Gospel is the solemn proclamation of the presence of the Son of God revealed in the flesh to renew a fallen world, to restore men from death to life." This tells of Jesus Christ, what he did, and what the results were: the Son of God renews a sinful world and restores us from death to life.

This is the gospel! These are "good and glad tidings, since they contain complete happiness." The kingdom of God has come in Christ and brought "a life of blessedness."

Among all the news and messages we encounter every day, we always need to focus on the most important news—the good news of the gospel of Jesus Christ. This message is at the core of our existence as disciples of Jesus Christ, children of God, and those filled with "the love of the Spirit" (Rom 15:30)!

HEBREWS 11:1-3

82

The Spirit Shows Us Hidden Things

The Spirit of God shows us hidden things, the knowledge of which cannot reach our senses.[83]

++++

On the meaning of faith, the writer of Hebrews memorably wrote: "Now faith is the assurance of things hoped for, the conviction of things not seen" (Heb 11:1).

When we think of faith, we often think of what we believe. Christian doctrine expresses the church's faith. It lays out important convictions that guide our believing and living as Christian persons. But "faith" also has personal dimensions that shape us every day. "Faith is the assurance of things hoped for," says the author of Hebrews. We have faith in God's promises and are assured of their reality and fulfillment in our lives. For example, the resurrection of Jesus assures us of our own resurrection—that's an assurance to which we hold on to by faith.

83. *Commentary on Hebrews 11:1.* CNTC 12:157.

Then, faith is "the conviction of things not seen." Faith is a reality that transcends what is around us at any given time. Faith surpasses our senses. Faith is a way of vision, of receiving deep convictions of realities that are not known in any other ways.

Faith is the work of God's Holy Spirit in our lives, in many ways. In the day-to-day, the Spirit shows us hidden things—the things that belong to faith and are known only in faith. As Calvin wrote, "The Spirit of God shows us hidden things, the knowledge of which cannot reach our senses."

A faith perspective can show us realities we would not otherwise know about. Faith sees beyond the "here and now" to future realities. These are presently hidden, but their truth and veracity are assured by the promises of God, which we receive in faith. "Hidden things" are revealed by the Spirit through faith. No situation is "impossible" because the Spirit is at work establishing and enacting faith. Faith assures us of God's presence and work with us, both now and in the future!

Hebrews 13:1-6

83

Receiving Christ in the Poor

We receive not only angels but Christ Himself when we receive the poor in His name.[84]

++++

In today's world, we are conditioned to be suspicious—even afraid—of "strangers." Those who are unknown to us cross our paths in various ways throughout our days. Mostly we "live and let live," going our own way and not going out of our way to offer ourselves to those not known to us.

But maybe we should not be in such a hurry to pass by the "stranger." The writer of Hebrews instructed: "Do not neglect to show hospitality to strangers, for by doing that some have entertained angels without knowing it" (Heb 13:2). The allusion here is probably to Abraham's experience of hospitably welcoming "three men"—and finding one of them was God, who promised Abraham

---

84. *Commentary on Hebrews 13:2*. CNTC 12:205.

and Sarah they would have a son (Genesis 18:1–15). Hospitality was an important practice for Old Testament Jews.

Here, there may also be an echo of Jesus' parable of the last judgment (Matt 25:31–46) when the King (Jesus) says that when one cares for the needs of others, "you do it to me" (25:45).

Thus, Calvin commented that "we receive not only angels but Christ Himself when we receive the poor in His name." When we are open, generous, and hospitable, extending care to others—even those we do not know, and especially those in need—we may be receiving "angels" and even *Jesus Christ himself*. In short, we never know in what way God may "visit" us through strangers and especially the poor and those in need.

This word should sharpen our sensitivities to welcoming others, both the stranger and the poor. They are those to whom "mutual love" can be given and shared (13:1). Our fears of others can be replaced by faith, and in all our interactions we can seek to share the love of Jesus Christ as we find ways to minister to and be ministered unto by others!

1 JOHN 4:7-12

84

Love Proves God Abides in Us

Love is the effect of the Spirit. . . . By His Spirit God abides in us. Therefore, by love we prove that we have God abiding in us. On the other hand, whoever claims to have God and does not love the brethren, shows his emptiness by this alone, for he separates God from himself.[85]

++++

First John says: "God is love" (1 John 4:8). We know this love by God sending Jesus Christ into the world "so that we might live through him" (4:9). From this deep love of God we recognize that "since God loved us so much, we also ought to love one another" (4:11). Though "no one has ever seen God, if we love one another, God lives in us, and his love is perfected in us" (4:12).

When we love one another, we know God's Spirit is living in us. As Calvin wrote, "Love is the effect of the Spirit. . . . By His Spirit God abides in us. Therefore, by love we prove that we have God abiding in us." When we show love we are sharing the love of

85. *Commentary on 1 John 4:12.* CNTC 5:293.

God living in us. In fact, we are never more like God than when we are loving others! Love is the test of our relationship with God and is the expression of God—through us—which extends to others.

"On the other hand," notes Calvin, "whoever claims to have God and does not love the brethren, shows his emptiness by this alone, for he separates God from himself." When we see members of the church failing to love, or acting in ways which are contrary to love, we are seeing people becoming estranged from God and quenching the Spirit of God who is to live in them.

We are to show the reality of God's continuing love in us. We share that love in ways that witness to God and meet human need. In this we are following Jesus Christ. Love proves God abides in us!

Selected Resources for Further Reflections

Battles, Ford Lewis. *The Piety of John Calvin: A Collection of His Spiritual Prose, Poems, and Hymns.* Reprint, Phillipsburg, NJ: P & R, 2009. Originally published as *The Piety of John Calvin: An Anthology Illustrative of the Spirituality of the Reformer.* Grand Rapids: Baker, 1978.

Calvin, John. *Calvin's Commentaries.* 45 vols. Edinburgh: Calvin Translation Society [CTS], 1844-56. Reprint in 22 vols. Grand Rapids: Baker, 1981.

———. *Calvin's New Testament Commentaries.* [CNTC] Edited by David W. Torrance and Thomas F. Torrance. Various Translators. 12 vols. Grand Rapids: Eerdmans, 1959-72.

———. *Institutes of the Christian Religion.* Edited by John T. McNeill; translated by Ford Lewis Battles. The Library of Christian Classics. Philadelphia: Westminster, 1960.

Gordon, Bruce. *Calvin.* New Haven, CT: Yale University Press, 2009.

Leith, John H. *John Calvin's Doctrine of the Christian Life.* Louisville: Westminster John Knox, 2006.

McKim, Donald K. "Calvin's View of Scripture." In *Readings in Calvin's Theology*, edited by Donald K. McKim, 43-68. Reprint. Eugene, OR: Wipf & Stock, 1998.

———. *Coffee with Calvin: Daily Devotions.* Louisville: Westminster John Knox, 2013.

———. *John Calvin: A Companion to His Life and Theology.* Eugene, OR: Cascade, 2015.

———. *The Westminster Dictionary of Theological Terms: Revised and Expanded, Second edition.* Louisville: Westminster John Knox, 2014.

McKim, Donald K., ed. *Calvin and the Bible.* New York: Cambridge University Press, 2006.

———, ed. *The Cambridge Companion to John Calvin.* New York: Cambridge University Press, 2004.

Selected Resources for Further Reflections

Rogers, Jack B., and Donald K. McKim. *The Authority and Interpretation of the Bible: An Historical Approach*. Reprint. Eugene, OR: Wipf & Stock, 1999.

Wallace, Ronald S. *Calvin's Doctrine of the Christian Life*. Reprint. Eugene, OR: Wipf & Stock, 1997.

Made in the USA
Columbia, SC
25 March 2024